PASSPORT TO SURVIVAL.

Four Survival Foods — Wheat, Powdered Milk, Honey and Salt

PASSPORT TO SURVIVAL

FOUR FOODS AND MORE TO USE AND STORE

BY ESTHER DICKEY

BOOKCRAFT INC.
SALT LAKE CITY, UTAH
1969

Library of Congress Catalog Card Number: 76-94979

13th Printing, 1973

LITHOGRAPHED IN U.S.A. BY

℗

PUBLISHERS PRESS
SALT LAKE CITY, UTAH

To my father,

ARTHUR W. ANDERSEN,

who at eighty-six still exemplifies cheerfulness,
courage, health and vitality, and who in matters
of both physical and spiritual health has been
my teacher and my inspiration.

Contents

Preface

The basic premise of this book is that for everyone, even for us who live in bounteous America, the time will probably come when food and other necessities are unobtainable. This situation may be brought about by any one of a number of causes —personal sickness or injury, unemployment, war, riot, transportation strikes, and so on. Our urban society is particularly vulnerable. Verlan Andersen sums it up in this way:

> With less than ten percent of the population engaged in farming and with this small group almost completely dependent upon a continuing supply of fuel, machinery, and smoothly functioning transportation network, famine could and would stalk the land within a matter of weeks if violence interrupted the operation of this highly interdependent system of food production and distribution . . . food markets would empty within hours and people would be left to their own devices to provide themselves with sustenance. The magnitude of the tragedy which could result is horrible to contemplate.[1]

The idea is not new. For years I have been reading and hearing counsel that families should prepare for such an eventuality by storing enough food and other necessities to last for twelve months. And during those years national and international conditions have worsened, making the threat more menacing.

But what foods shall we store for family needs? How can we, on the most economical basis, store foods which not only can help to ensure our healthy survival in time of famine or other emergency but can be rotated to provide good meals in normal times and thus avoid spoilage?

I was steered toward the answer by early training and environment in the shape of a wise father—a wheat grower and

---

[1]H. Verlan Andersen, *Many Are Called but Few Are Chosen* (Provo, Utah: Press Publishing Co., 1967).

producer of honey who also had a considerable knowledge of
soils, of plant and animal life, and of bodily needs for health.
My later reading, observation and experiment confirmed the
validity of that earlier experience and helped me to establish for
myself as the fundamental storage items the four "emergency"
foods — wheat, powdered milk, honey, and salt. This book deals
principally with the storage of these four items and their use in
providing appetizing meals in normal times in preparation for
a survival diet.

This is not a conventional cookbook. Nor is it a book on
nutrition, for I am not professionally trained in that field. The
value of *Passport to Survival* is that it gives guidance on food
preparation, preservation and storage which is based upon many
years of my own observation, experience and experiment. Some
of the experience was costly, as learning often is. In much of the
experimentation, success was achieved only after failures. All
the recipes in this book have been tried out successfully on my
own family. The creative, "just-for-fun" ideas given, no less than
the more down-to-earth meals, demonstrate the value and versatility of the four foods.

Over the years it has been my privilege and opportunity to
demonstrate the value and versatility of the four survival foods
before numerous groups in many parts of America and even over-
seas. Everywhere I have found an enthusiastic response. Everywhere I have been urged to make the material available in print
so that housewives can experience the confidence which comes
first from storing the four foods, and then turning those foods
over in the challenge and enjoyment of preparing appetizing and
interesting meals. This book is an attempt to satisfy that expressed demand as well as the unconscious need shared by the
many who have not as yet come into contact with the survival diet.

While the four survival foods constitute the emphasis and
main part of this book, certain other aspects of survival are
discussed to the extent necessary to give reasonable balance to
the subject within the compass of a moderately sized book.
(I have not attempted to deal with preparation for an enemy
attack, since at least ten publications on shelters, protection
against radioactive fallout, etc., are available free from local Civil
Defense Offices.) Some references for further study are given in
chapter 18. I may say that while physical nourishment is obvi-

ously of the highest priority to survival, remaining alive without faith, courage, cheerfulness, and a hope of a better future is but to exist in a way which severely debases the value of the survival. The brief space accorded to this subject in the book is no gauge of the vital importance of positive, enthusiastic living, whether under normal or survival conditions.

Members of audiences at demonstrations I have presented have offered ideas and suggestions which are incorporated in this book, and for these I am grateful as I share them with readers. Since I expect to continue learning throughout life, the book is obviously not the last word on the subjects discussed. Rather, it is to be hoped that, like the demonstrations, it will stimulate further ideas, modifications, and improvements.

In producing this book I would like to express my appreciation

— To my husband, Russell F. Dickey, for his patience, encouragement, and help in developing the recipes.

— To my family, for their creative ideas and for sampling my food "experiments."

— To Jack West, who originated the idea of the four survival foods.

— To my son, Neldon, whose idea it was to package the four foods in a five-gallon can.

— To my parents, Arthur W. and Clara Andersen, for the deep understanding of health and nourishment they have shared with me.

— To members of my family and relatives for encouragement and assistance in preparing the manuscript: K. J. and Amelia Andersen, Mark and Joyce Andersen, Richard and Dorene Landolfe, Ruth Laughlin, Robert and Gladys Stum, Scott and Beth Whitaker, and Annette Burton.

— To George Bickerstaff, senior editor at Bookcraft, Inc., for his painstaking effort in editing and organizing this work.

— To Kent C. Esplin, owner of Perma-Pak, for his critical reading of and helpful suggestions on the manuscript.

— To Lee Irwin, Dr. James A. Owen, Dr. Rodney I. Palmer, M.D., K. Ellsworth Payne, Utahna Kerr, Verla Jeffries,

Geri Van Zyl, Carol Lynn Wright, William Allen, Stanley Nuffer, Jeannine Burt, William E. Holmes, and Stanley and Christine Jones, for help given in various ways.

— To many others not mentioned by name, but who helped to make this book possible.

Most of all I express appreciation to our God and Creator who has given us life and has graciously provided us with Nature's means to sustain and develop it. In all our planning for survival or for anything else we will do well to acknowledge this fact with gratitude.

PART I

FOODS FOR
HEALTHY SURVIVAL

CHAPTER 1

Nightmare Day

In the 1940's George Orwell wrote a fascinating if grim story entitled *Nineteen Eighty-Four*. In it he projected in imagination the international situation at that future time and the way of life in one of the super-states of the day—a life in which not only personal actions but even thoughts are subject to a rigid control under an iron dictatorship which is supported by an advanced science and technology. As one reads the book and identifies with the main character one seems almost to be experiencing a nightmare.

Perhaps such depressing and calamitous predictions will not materialize, but there are other nightmare possibilities ahead, particularly in the field of food supply. America's vast food surpluses have been drastically reduced; strikes threaten distribution; civil disorder and lawlessness menace our society; and despite the nuclear nonproliferation treaty, nuclear weapons and their awesome means of delivery multiply. Any or all of these factors could bring, long before that actual year, our own nightmare "1984" — a nightmare of famine and, for the unprepared, deprivation and even starvation.

To dramatize this situation, share with me this bad dream— a dream so vivid and real that you cannot get it off your mind. In the dream you are in a market with your basket and grocery list. A sick feeling comes over you as you look down the aisles and see row after row of grocery shelves almost empty. You have eight items on your shopping list, but only two are available, and these are the least essential. There is not even a loaf of bread in the store, nor any milk.

Having five children to feed, you are overcome with panic. You rush home and sit in the chair by the window—frustrated, bewildered, worn out. Looking across the street you see a whole family arriving at the Taylors'. They are walking. The older boy is carrying the baby on his back, and everyone has big bundles—

clothes and other portable necessities, probably. Mrs. Taylor takes them all in the house.

In the way dreams have of mixing general impressions and specific detail, you get a feeling of overall confusion and uncertainty. The Paulsons, who have farmed their land in peace for fifty years, are besieged with people who trample over their fields stealing their cabbage and squash. Goods are being stolen from the stores, markets and schools are closed, many people are out of work. The car is out of gas and your husband rides your son's bicycle looking for work. You are told there are carrots and potatoes available further out in the country, and since there is almost no food in the house you decide to walk there. You search among all your shoes for sturdy oxfords to walk in but can't find any. You feel trapped, with your husband and the children home and not knowing from one meal to the next what to give them to eat.

Your mind flashes constantly to something new to worry about—like winter coming, a cold house, oil tank empty, furnace silent, the wood supply for the fireplace almost depleted. You worry about the children getting sick and what you'd do if you couldn't get an appointment with the doctor, who is working to the breaking point already with all the sickness in town.

Depressing visions of Thanksgiving day and Christmas flood your mind. The children are fretting and unhappy because the family can't spend either of these occasions with their grandparents. You think of past Thanksgiving and Christmas holidays when happy times and delicious dinners were taken for granted.

Mrs. Taylor has brought you a few candles because she has heard the warning about the electricity being temporarily shut off. She advises you to store drinking water, and you are filling what empty fruit jars and bottles you can find. As you talk with this good neighbor you are amazed at how strong she is— a little more serious than usual, but energetic and determined. You are very thankful to have her for a neighbor.

But still your mind reverts to Christmas, only weeks away. You stand as if in a trance. How could life change so much from one year to another? Where will you get the courage to be cheerful and make this a happy occasion for your family? You feel as if you are in a deep, black hole with no way out.

While you may not personally have had this nightmare, your experience with dreams helps you to know the sense of relief one would have on waking from it. Fortunately there is food in your cupboard, gas in the car; and your husband and the children are going to work and school as usual.

But don't feel *too* relieved. The nightmare might still arrive for many of us, and this time *in reality*. For many years people have been strongly urged to store food and other necessities in their homes, against any one or a combination of the several possible emergencies—unemployment, sickness, strikes, famine, civil disorder, war, and so on. To be unprepared despite the repeated warnings would certainly increase the nightmare quality of the experience.

Perhaps for most of us there is still time, if we procrastinate no further. On the basis of my own experience, with its trials and errors, successes and failures, I suggest as a beginning the concepts, foods and methods outlined in the pages of this book.

CHAPTER 2

The Four Survival Foods

Conscious of my lack of professional training in nutrition, I approach this chapter with considerable humility. Here I attempt only a general presentation, and this primarily on the basis of (1) what seems to me the most remarkable composition and usability characteristics of the four foods, wheat, milk, honey, and salt; (2) the historical background of these foods, which indicates their particular adaptability to man's nutrition; and (3) the proclamation of contemporary nutritionists that whole grains and milk products, along with fresh fruits and vegetables, should dominate one's diet.

USABILITY AND STORABILITY

As will be extended later in this book, the versatility of these four foods by which they can be modified, combined, and recombined to give variety and palatable food preparations seems almost never-ending. It is my personal findings in these directions which have been the major motivation of this book; it is my personal conviction that in these foods lie the basic components of an emergency survival diet.

Wheat

Upon examining the voluminous nutritional charts of food analysis, one finds wide variation in food composition relative to amino acids (proteins), fats, carbohydrates, and minerals and vitamins. It is obvious that, depending on the component chosen as an index, foods will vary in their ratings in respect to each other. When we choose one index, a particular food will be high on a generalized list; when we choose another index the same food may be low. For instance, beef protein is said to be superior to wheat protein, as it contains a higher percentage of the amino acid, lysine, than does wheat protein. Conversely, however, wheat protein contains more of the amino acid, phenyl alanine, than does beef protein, and one could argue greater virtues for wheat on this latter basis.

A basic evaluation of nutritional qualifications which is often overlooked in nutrition relates to the quantity of a particular food consumed. Here again we may compare wheat with meat. Whereas for economic reasons meat is generally consumed sparingly, wheat often represents a major percentage of the diet. Thus even though the lysine content may be somewhat lower in wheat than in meat, this would normally be more than compensated for by the larger quantity of wheat consumed.

Irrespective of the nutritional value of wheat as shown by chemical composition tables, wheat is one of the most highly rated foods from the standpoint of "biological value." This value is determined by animal experimentation and relates to the percentage of protein utilization under controlled conditions. On this basis the following list gives the generally accepted comparative ratings of the more common protein foods in their unprocessed state:

> Eggs (whole)
> Milk (whole)
> Meat (beef, fish)
> Rice (whole)
> Wheat (whole)
> Potatoes (white)
> Oats (whole)
> Barley (whole)
> Corn (whole)
> Rye (whole)
> Peas and Beans (dried)

Through various degrees of processing, the relative positions of these items can be significantly changed. If only the wheat germ of wheat is considered, it takes a place in the list between meat and rice. If soybean meal is considered, it occupies a position next to wheat, but when evaluated on the basis of the whole seed (even though it has an exceptionally high percentage of protein) it drops further down the list. It is seen then that the nutritional value changes as the initial foodstuff is subjected to processing. Another example is that soybeans *per se* contain about 35 percent protein. When part of the oils are removed, the protein percentage jumps to 43 percent.

Yet another index enters into the evaluation of foodstuffs for a survival diet. This relates to storability. Upon examination of the above list, one asks, "Why not store rice?" The answer is simple. Whole rice — and this is a peculiar quirk of Nature — simply does not store. Even in sealed containers, it becomes rancid in as short a time as a year and a half. If one thus eliminates whole rice, wheat remains the highest rated grain on the list. (Polished rice appropriately protected against weevils is an excellent storable food and will keep for many years.) Hard wheat and corn are the best storing grains, and fortunately for survival diets they are near the top of the list in nutritional value.

Powdered Milk

To some, the mere mention of the second food, powdered milk, evokes disapproval This feeling usually stems from previous experiences with reconstituted low-fat powdered milk, wherein its flavor has been unconsciously compared with that of fresh whole milk. But a more objective evaluation is needed, and this reveals that the flavor of properly prepared, good quality powdered milk is acceptable in itself, and in fact differs only slightly from that of fresh skim milk. (Instant powdered milk may differ to a greater extent than non-instant.) Furthermore, substantial evidence (including actual samples) is available that fat-free powdered milk, when kept dry and reasonably cool, stores with little change for over 15 years. Such credentials rate this commodity high on the list of storage items. Its status soars to even greater heights when one refers back to the biological value chart and finds that milk is listed virtually at the top of the list as a protein food. Certainly by storing this high-ranking animal protein food and the high-ranking grain, wheat, each of which has a high rating of storability, one lays a firm and substantial foundation for emergency nutrition.

Honey

Upon first examining nutritional charts for the food value of honey, the third item of the four listed emergency foods, one is tempted to regard this as just another high-sugar content food and to discount the many historical claims as to its virtues. Perhaps this would be unjust to honey, even though some exaggerated claims are made for it.

The nature of the sugar content of honey has led many would-be nutritionists astray. Honey is composed of two sugars, levulose (fructose) and glucose (dextrose), the two prominent sugars contained in blood. Many have incorrectly argued that this gives particular virtue to honey. The saliva of man contains a potent enzyme (the same as the bees) which transforms table sugar (saccharose/sucrose) efficiently and rapidly to exactly the same combination of sugars as is found in honey. Therefore, the diabetic, for example, metabolizes honey in exactly the same way he does table sugar. Both foods result in the same percentage of fructose and glucose. From all indications, the nectar of flowers consists of sucrose. Whether the bee or human saliva effects the transformation to simpler sugars, the stomach receives identically the same amount of sugar combination and in turn passes the mixture along the digestive tract on the pathway toward the blood stream. Thus the only advantage of honey over table sugar for the diabetic is that honey is sweeter than table sugar, and this encourages smaller consumption. May I add that this advantage applies also to the non-diabetic, especially in the United States where excessive sugar consumption is a universal dietary defect.

For myself, I find there is much to recommend honey. First there is its unique flavor. To my mind, as a sweetener honey makes an unequalled contribution to an emergency diet. On bread and in cereals, cookies, and homemade candy it cannot be superseded by any other food product without sacrifice of palatability. But honey has other virtues, too. As it is essentially a concentrated extract from the plant kingdom, it undoubtedly contains numerous minor components which contribute in some degree to man's nutrition. It will come as a surprise to many to learn that a tablespoonful of honey contains as much vitamin C as a medium-sized apple, and that this same quantity has three times as much iron as the apple. It also possesses the same quantity of protein and nicotinic acid as the apple and a somewhat higher content of riboflavin.[1] Nevertheless it must be recognized that honey, like the apple, is far from a complete food. Its greatest virtue lies in its pleasing flavor.

---

[1] Information as shown in Heinz Nutritional Charts.

Salt

There remains the fourth item on my list, salt. It is questionable whether this particular substance should actually be classified as a food. In reality it is a mineral, a chemical combination of sodium and chlorine. It is not metabolized to yield energy, nor does it seem to be related to static structures of the body. It is a dynamic entity constantly being shifted from one body cell compartment to another. It is involved in almost all cellular processes. Because of this constant movement it is susceptible to loss during certain body conditions and therefore requires replenishment through the food. Its loss is also caused by an unbalanced diet consisting mostly of fruits and vegetables. This is strikingly evidenced in the well recognized distribution of salt to range cattle. Similarly blocks of salt are placed in high mountain areas to maintain the health of wild deer. It is potassium salts (not sodium chloride) which predominate in plant food, and the exclusive consumption of such food is one of the primary causes leading to salt (sodium chloride) depletion on vegetarian diets.

Wheat and Milk — High Nutritional Value

I have referred somewhat to the nutritional aspects of honey and salt. Let us now return for a more detailed examination of wheat and milk. Nutritional charts reveal hard wheat to contain about 75 percent carbohydrate, 12-16 percent protein, about 1.7 percent fat, and the balance water. The ratios may vary to some extent depending on the variety of wheat and the locality in which it was grown, but the composition generally remains within this range. As we have previously seen, wheat protein is of high nutritional quality. This supplemented with milk proteins places the proposed survival foods in one of the highest nutritional categories.

The carbohydrate fraction of wheat consists of readily digestible starch in appropriate proportion. The fat content is mostly of the more preferable unsaturated variety, also in an appropriate proportion. The fat appears to be retained primarily in the wheat germ. From a storage standpoint the most labile food is fat, and most fats and oils become rancid within a few months. But, remarkably, the unbroken wheat kernel possesses the capacity to retain its fat (oil) for scores of years with no detectable change. The secret of this probably lies in the antioxidant characteristics of vitamin E (alpha-tocopherol). Some success has been attained in the commercial storage of fats by supplementary addition of this vitamin, but the acme of success has been achieved by Nature in the wheat kernel. It is the wheat germ portion of the wheat kernel where most of the fat and vitamin E is located. This is also the area especially rich in members of the B complex vitamins. Vitamin B_1 and nicotinic acid predominate, but riboflavin B_2 is present in moderate quantities. Vitamins A and C are lacking. But here resides another remarkable trait of wheat. When the wheat kernel is allowed to germinate, the latter vitamins are synthesized and the content of the B vitamins is sharply increased.

The art (science) of seed sprouting is only recently beginning to unfold. Experiments have been carried out at several universities, and reports in the scientific literature are rapidly increasing. Sprouted seeds during times of food shortage have been introduced into the diet under a variety of circumstances and indicate most promising potential. Catharyn Elwood, in her book *Feel Like a Million!* (published by The Devin-Adair Company), relates the results of experiments involving British, Indian and Serbian troops which showed not only that sprouted seeds were highly successful in removing the symptoms of scurvy, but that they were more effective for this purpose than lemon juice.

Catharyn Elwood's book contains an extensive review of various studies which have shown a rapid and striking up-step of vitamin content during the germination process. For example, England, which is dependent on outside sources for fresh fruit to supply vitamin C, has made special studies of the vitamin C content of sprouted grains and has found that about 2 oz. (50 grams) of peas sprouted for 48 hours or 1 oz. sprouted for 96 hours amply supplies the daily vitamin C requirement. Dr. W. C. Bailey of the University of Minnesota reports large increases in the B vitamins in sprouted wheat. For details of these and other findings, and indications of how the sprouting time affects the vitamin content, the reader is referred to Catharyn Elwood's book.

Although modern nutrition seems to be expounding the virtues of individual food components, it seems to have accomplished little improvement over that of the original products of Nature.

Whole grains still retain the spotlight in their contribution of the B vitamins, and these, as we have seen, are greatly increased in wheat during sprouting. In addition, vitamins lacking in the original seed suddenly come into being during sprouting, thus enhancing the value of this already excellent food.

Vitamin E is another attribute of the wheat germ. Its role as an antioxidant in protecting the wheat germ oil against rancidity was referred to above. Additionally there are significant scientific findings from animal experiments with this vitamin which indicate profound implications for human nutrition, and numerous reports to the same effect are appearing in medical journals. It now appears likely that vitamin E relates to the reproduction system in both males and females, influences the fetus, muscle tissue, blood formation, and certain tissues related to the nervous system. A recent review by the Nutrition Foundation Inc., N. Y., "Present Knowledge of Nutrition," references numerous papers from competent research establishments which clearly implicate vitamin E in human nutrition.

FOUR FOODS ARE TIME-PROVEN

A strong case for the four emergency foods can be presented on grounds of historical background. Wheat is constantly referred to in written history as "the staff of life." Land "flowing with milk and honey" and salt with good "savor" was a continual dream of the ancients. With their freedom from the physical distractions which we have about us today and their constant awareness of the hardships in obtaining sufficient to eat, food was always in the foreground of their thought. It is said that reference to "a land flowing with milk and honey" is mentioned in the Bible seventy times. Food is the subject of many episodes in the scriptures. Ruth, a gleaner in the fields of Boaz, gathered wheat for Naomi and herself. Journeys to different lands during famine occurred frequently. Poetic descriptions of flowing fields of grain, the whiteness of milk, the sweetness of honey, abound in the scriptures.

We can truthfully say that man owes a great deal of his existence through the ages to these particular foodstuffs. But more than this we can say that time has proven their adaptability to the nutrition of man. They are, in simple language, time-proven.

Contemporary Nutritional Findings

The third listed justification I gave at the beginning of this chapter for my confidence in these foodstuffs was that of their acceptance in contemporary nutritional recommendations. At the time of the writing of this book (1969), several surveys have been published relative to the current nutritional status of people of the United States. Appallingly, the Department of Agriculture finds 50 percent of American families, rich and poor alike, existing (subsisting) on inadequate diets. It was found that 37 percent of the families with incomes of $10,000 or more had diets which were below standard in one or more of seven different categories.

It is evident that greater use of milk and whole wheat would eliminate a major part of the nutritional problems of the United States, and these two foodstuffs are the basis for my survival diet. Insufficient consumption of fresh fruit and vegetables, another inadequacy of the current American diet, is not so easily remedied in emergency conditions. I make no suggestion that the emergency four can compete with the great variety of fresh vegetables and fruits flowing year round from the fields and orchards of our land. However, remember we are concerned in this book principally with a survival diet. Where do we turn if the flow of fresh foods suddenly (or gradually) stops? Atomic fall-out, transportation failure, crop failure or food-handler strikes are but a few possibilities to cause such a condition. I simply say that a significant contribution to the vitamin C and A requirements of human nutrition can be supplied to the diet through sprouting wheat and various seeds as recommended in this book. Both sprouts and wheat grass are greatly up-stepped in their content of these two critical vitamins when compared to the original seed.

Thus it is these four emergency foods, wheat, milk powder, honey and salt — nutritionally sound, readily storable, highly adaptable and pleasingly palatable — in which I place my trust as the basis of my passport to survival.

CHAPTER 3

Survival Four and Forty More

When I go shopping today, on the shelves of the supermarket there are literally thousands of items to choose from. A minimum figure is eight thousand, and one source puts it at thirty thousand. Which of these many items should I include in my personal storage plan? Since my family are accustomed to so many different foods, I am afraid they might murmur a little if it became necessary to feed them on just the survival four for an extended period. More variety is clearly desirable.

From a chart listing 155 common foods I selected about 40 for my personal storage plan. The chart rated the foods as to vitamin and mineral content, and the forty I chose were rated high. Other factors in my choice were that the forty were economical to buy and would store well. I listed them in groups which reflect a descending order of nutritional value, striving for a balance between proteins, fats, carbohydrates, and vitamins and minerals.

Now I had scaled down the 8,000 to 30,000 food items to a more manageable number. These I could categorize so that I knew something of their respective values in the family diet. I felt that I could eat these foods now, and that they would keep me well until I'm a hundred — emergency or not! I felt secure.

I have good reasons for selecting each item on the list, but let me particularly mention five items which rate high in my personal storage plan.

Peanut butter. I put peanut butter next after the survival four foods because all my family like it, it is a ready-to-eat food, it is high in protein and fat, and its flavor is compatible with the survival four. However, it does not store well and must be rotated.

Tomato juice. We like it. It has a relatively large vitamin C and vitamin A content. The color of tomato juice is tempting, and the juice would provide some liquid in the event of a water shortage.

Soybeans. I can't claim soybeans as a family favorite, but they get priority because of their high nutritive value. They have a higher mineral content than most grains and legumes. They are about 30 to 50 percent protein, which compares with about 12 percent in wheat and about 35 percent in meat for comparable weights. From about 12 to 25 percent of the soybean is oil.

Blackstrap Molasses. This is another flavor and cooking food. It adds greatly to flavor variety when used with the survival four. Also, it contains appreciable quantities of calcium, phosphorous and iron.

Dried green peas. These contain significant quantities of vitamin A and of the vitamin B complex. They contain also the minerals potassium, magnesium, iron, phosphorus, and sulfur in appreciable quantities. Dried green peas are quite inexpensive, costing only a few cents a pound when bought in 100-pound quantities at feed stores. (Be sure they do not contain pesticides.)

Below I list the foods included in my personal storage plan, including the survival four. These foods, supplemented with fresh vegetables and fruits as available, are my choice for an economical and nutritive diet with favorable storage qualities.

Foods I Store

(Categories listed in descending order of importance
in my food storage plan.)

1. Four survival foods which will keep indefinitely when stored properly:

    Wheat   Honey
    Powdered milk   Salt

2. Three valuable additions to the above four which require rotation:

    Peanut butter
    Tomato juice   Vitamin pills

3. Nine other foods high in nutritive value which require rotation:

Soybeans   Blackstrap molasses
Lentils   Brown rice
Dried green peas   Dry yeast (I store ¾
Millet   pound a person)
Yellow corn   Vegetable powders

4. Six foods that will keep for from three to five years:

Canned meat   Rice polishings
Figs   Sauerkraut
Rye (will keep longer   Canned tomatoes
   than five years)

5. Five foods that will keep for from one to three years:

Dried fruit[1]   Evaporated milk
Vegetable oil (Normally I   Raisins
   do not use shortening)   String beans (fermented)

6. Other foods it is nice to have on hand:

Nuts and nut butter[2]

A freezer-full of meat (have a way to smoke the meat if
electricity becomes unavailable)

Compact items to store for use with the survival four:
Bouillon cubes, onion flakes, dry soup mix, sesame seeds
(high in protein, calcium, vitamins B and E), alfalfa
seed (to sprout, for salads), and paprika[2] (which contains a concentrated natural source of vitamin C)

Dry grated cheese,[2] garlic, mushroom soup, gravy mix, and
meat seasonings (to make wheat main dishes more
tempting)

Vanilla, almond flavoring, cinnamon, nutmeg, food coloring, and rennet tablets (to help change the flavor and
appearance of plain food)

Gelatin dessert, pineapple (juice[2] and slices), dates, and
prunes (to add variety to meals)

---

[1]"Low-moisture" fruits dried commercially will keep from 5 to 10 years.
[2]Do not store well.

CHAPTER 4

Emergency Diet in Action

When I reached the point of having a good supply of emergency foods in store the next question was what to do with them. Clearly it is no use waiting for an emergency before discovering how to use the food.

I found that the transition from a normal to an emergency diet, should that become necessary, need not be the calamity most people would expect it to be — especially if the housewife has included the storage foods in her day-to-day planning of meals during normal times and is therefore familiar with their use.

During a ten-day trial period I prepared meals for my family using nothing but the four survival foods — wheat, milk, honey and salt. It wasn't the dismal experience many would suppose. We all felt well and our meals were interesting. In the light of this admittedly limited experience and of the research I have done I make the following observations on what I could expect if my family were to go on the survival-four diet for an extended period.

Bulk in the diet. Here is a comparison, by weight, of the amounts of food consumed monthly by the average person in America on the normal as opposed to the emergency diet.

Normal Diet	*Emergency Diet*
25 lb. meat and potatoes (12½ lb. of each) plus approximately 153 lb. of additional food	27 lb. wheat (substitute for meat and potatoes) plus 3 lb. honey, 5 lb. dry milk and up to 1 lb. salt

From this it seems that, although we would not have nutritional hunger on the emergency diet, we would miss the bulky fruits and vegetables. I expected to lose weight during the ten-day experimental period, but I did not. Of course, the matter of loss of weight on this diet would depend on such factors as a person's normal weight, usual food consumption, physical activity, and so on.

Water-free storage foods do not provide the bulk we are accustomed to in our diet — some of the solid foods we normally eat, such as potatoes and apples, are over 50 percent water. (One advantage of sprouting wheat — see chapter 5 — is that it greatly increases its bulk.) The table below compares the bulk in the normal diet with that in the emergency diet, on a daily, monthly, and yearly basis. It reminds us again of the need to store water.

Pounds of Food Per Person

	Normal Diet	Emergency Diet
Day	6	1.2
Month	178	36
Year	2,136	432

Calories. Calorie requirements vary with such factors as age, sex, and occupation. An approximate figure for men aged forty-five is 3,000 calories a day, and for women the same age, 2,200. Children aged one to three need about 1,300 calories a day. The average daily calorie intake on the normal diet is about 2,000, and the comparison with the emergency diet is as follows:

Normal Diet	Emergency Diet
2,000 calories a day	1,864 calories a day

The book *Slim, Trim, Fun for Life,* by Sara Lee Gibb (published by Bookcraft) contains useful tables listing the nutritive values of about five hundred foods. From such tables it is not difficult to draw up a list of foods which ensure a high level of nutrition and at the same time exercise control as to calorie intake. The emergency diet will be found to compare favorably with such a diet as to calorie and protein intake in particular, as well as to cost.

Proteins. Protein needs are a major concern in relation to an emergency diet. It was therefore reassuring for me to see whole wheat high on the list of protein foods rated according to biological value. (See chapter 2.)

The following figures show recommended daily amounts of protein:

Men	70 grams	Girls 16-19	75 grams
Women	58 grams	Children 4-6	50 grams
Boys 16-19	100 grams		

How does the emergency diet measure up against these needs? Hard wheat which is 12 percent protein contains 54.48 grams of protein per pound (2½ cups). Regular dry, skim milk powder contains 41.2 grams of protein to every 4 ounces (1 cup). On the basis of these figures, the amount of protein obtained daily from the emergency diet is as follows:

Amount of Food	Grams of Protein
2¼ cups of wheat	49.04
⅔ cup of regular dry skim milk powder	27.03
Total	76.07

Iron. Whole wheat is a good source of iron. Where the body needs a high intake of iron, as with those suffering from anemia, one can draw upon other iron-rich storage foods such as dried green peas, beans, lentils, corn, dried fruit, nuts and molasses. In addition, a small garden plot can provide vegetables having a high iron content — e.g., string beans, parsley, and Swiss chard.

Cost. During my ten-day trial period the cost of the food I prepared was less than 25 cents a day for each person. Where else would one obtain for such a small cost a diet which is satisfying, interesting, varied, and nutritious? (I note that the average United States family with a yearly income of $6,000 spends about $3.50 a day on food.)

Variety. While my experiment used only the four survival foods, I am sure that these would tend to get monotonous over a long period, since we are accustomed to the wide variety of foods available in the markets. Obviously the housewife would need a whole bag of tricks to help her vary the meals she would be preparing. I hope that this book, and particularly chapters 5-8, will supply the basis and the motivation for the beginning collection of aids to this variety.

BABIES AND THE EMERGENCY DIET

At the time of my experiment there was no one in my family who was still in the baby stage. What if there had been? In an emergency situation could babies eat the four survival foods? The following information should put Mother's mind at ease on this matter.

Roughage. While mothers are accustomed to giving their babies soft, bland foods, Dr. D. T. Quigley, M.D., points out the need for roughage in their diet:

> The most common disorder among babies is constipation, due to lack of bulk in the diet . . . to suggest that a baby can take fresh vegetables and whole wheat along with meat sounds impossible to the person who has had the need for giving baby "gentle" foods drummed into them. Actually children thrive on it if they are started on small quantities and their tolerance is not exceeded.[1]

Since the digestive capacity for babies is not as great as that of adults, the food, whether it be cooked wheat (see #48 E), sprouts, gluten, or breads, would of course need to be softened for infants without teeth.

Honey. Some doctors recommend honey to sweeten the baby's formula. Use 1 or 2 teaspoons to an 8-oz. bottle of milk. Honey acts as a mild laxative. If baby is constipated, increase the honey by ½ teaspoon; if his bowel movements are loose, decrease the honey by that amount. Babies on honey rarely have colic. Minerals in the honey provide the infant with part of his needs in this respect as the body grows.

Wheat grass and wheat sprouts. Adding wheat grass juice to the baby's milk formula would increase the intake of vitamins C, A and E. Wheat sprouts (also alfalfa sprouts, mung

---

[1] D. T. Quigley, *The National Malnutrition* (Milwaukee: Olsen Publishing Co., 1952) p. 100.

bean sprouts, etc.) could be liquified and fed to a baby until he is old enough to masticate the food.

Nutritious broth. Warm water poured over wheat bran (or barley, millet or oats) and allowed to stand overnight, then poured off, sweetened with honey and given to the baby would supply added minerals and vitamins and proteins.

Milk. A baby who is taking insufficient liquid milk could be fed a pudding made from milk and honey. (#80, chapter 6.)

Wheat pudding. Steamed cooked wheat, mixed in the blender with milk and honey and then strained, makes a soft pudding.

PART II

RECIPES AND MENUS

CHAPTER 5

Survival-Four Recipes

To the housewife who is accustomed to providing major portions of the meal by opening cans of pre-cooked food and quickly heating the contents, our storage foods cannot be recommended on grounds of convenience. I take it, however, that anyone using this book will not rate convenience on the same level as nutritional value and preparation for emergency. And certainly many appetizing meals can be prepared by combining our survival four with other foods and seasonings.

In this and the following chapter are over a hundred recipes which require only wheat, powdered milk, honey, and salt, with suggested seasonings and other additions where these are available. In this present chapter let's learn to prepare plain, basic foods. Later we can let the imagination take wings.

Here, then, are ways of preparing these basic foods:

Cooked wheat
Sprouts
Wheat grass
Wild yeast
Sourdough bread
Batter and dough (unleavened)
Gluten
Milk-and-honey sweet base

For your guidance I have also added information on making bread and on weights, measures and temperatures used in cooking the survival four.

COOKED WHEAT

Knowledge of how to cook wheat in a variety of ways may prove helpful in emergency conditions. Therefore, try several methods — use an open pot, double boiler, improvised steamer, thermos jug, pressure cooker; or try canning the way you can beans at the custom cannery or in jars at home.

Note that more of the food value is retained with lower-temperature than with higher-temperature methods. (Wheat cooked for 14 hours in a stainless steel pan on "simmer" in the top of a double boiler was planted, and it grew!) Whatever method is used, start by adding cold water to the grain, then bring it to a boil.

The proportion used is usually two parts water to one part grain. (Use less water for the steam method — 3½ parts water to 2½ parts grain.)

The method will depend on available fuel, containers, and stoves. (About two-thirds of the world's women still cook over open fires, a method which would make it difficult to keep wheat on simmer all night.) When fuel was scarce, one ingenious family collected enough chips to make a fire and boil water, poured the boiling water over the wheat in a pan, added a tight lid and buried the pan in the haystack overnight. Another family, this one in wartime Holland, poured boiling water over the wheat, added a tight lid to the pan, wrapped the pan in several thicknesses of newspaper and put it under the bedcovers overnight. In both instances the insulation was sufficient to retain the heat, and by morning the wheat was cooked and ready for breakfast.

#1. STEAMED WHEAT

For plump, fluffy, separate grains, cook by surrounding the kernels with live steam. This takes a combination of pans, one inside the other. Cook plenty of wheat and use it all the week. You will need:

5 cups wheat	perforated rack to fit in the
7 cups water	larger pan and support
1 tbs. salt	the smaller pan (three
small open pan or casserole	perforated cans with top
larger pan	and bottom removed will
	suffice)

Put the ingredients in the small pan (or casserole) and set it on the rack in the larger pan. Pour water in the large pan to the level of an inch below the bottom of the small pan. Cover large pan and steam for 4 hours. Reduce heat after first 15 minutes.

Equipment for Steaming Wheat

The starch granules in the wheat will swell or burst and completely absorb the 7 cups of water. Twelve cups of steamed wheat will result. About half the water in the larger pan will be converted into steam during the cooking. (*Note*: For smaller recipes use 2 cups wheat, 1¾ cups water, 1 tsp. salt. Makes 5 cups steamed wheat.)

The steamed method is faster than the double boiler method, and the resultant kernels are softer. On one occasion I soaked wheat for 8 hours and then cooked it in a double boiler for another 8 hours, and at the end of this time it was not as soft as wheat I had steamed for 4 hours without giving it any previous soaking.

#2. THERMOS-COOKED WHEAT

1 cup wheat   1 tsp. salt

Soak wheat for 10 hrs. in just enough water to cover it. Drain off water into a measured container, adding enough water to make 2 cups. Add salt and soaked grain and bring to visible boil. Pour into pre-heated one-quart thermos bottle. Tightly cap bottle and turn it on side. Leave for about 10 hours.

#3. CRACKED WHEAT (double boiler)

1 cup cracked (coarsely-   3 cups water
    ground) wheat   1 tsp. salt

Bring water and salt to rolling boil. Sprinkle wheat in, to avoid lumping. Cook in the top of a double boiler for about 1 hour.

#4. BULGAR WHEAT

2 cups wheat   1 tsp. salt
2 cups water

Steam for 45 minutes. Spread the cooked wheat on a cookie sheet in a single layer. Dry out completely in a 200° oven (takes about 1 hour). (If desired, wet surface of dried wheat slightly and rub kernels between hands to loosen and remove chaff.) Store the processed bulgar in a jar. Use it whole, or crack it in mill or grinder.

When preparing it for use, boil or steam it from 10 to 20 minutes.

SPROUTING

For a new adventure in eating, try sprouting seeds, grains, and nuts. On the four-food survival plan, sprouting the wheat is necessary for a nutritionally adequate diet. Note too that all dried foods cook faster if they are first sprouted — kidney beans, for example, cook in about 30 minutes, an important consideration in time of fuel scarcity or even in the modern kitchen. Additionally, sprouting beans before cooking them eliminates the usual after-effects of stomach gas.

The nutritive value of sprouted grains, seeds and beans, and the relatively small storage space they require, make these very good storage items.

A miracle takes place when grain sprouts. All man has to do is to provide moisture, warmth and air, and the dormant kernel, the storehouse of nutrition that feeds the plant, comes to life.

In sprouting wheat there are three major factors to consider:

1. Proper conditions for germination.
2. Type of container required.
3. Stage at which sprouts are best for eating.

Conditions. Pick out broken seeds because they tend to mold rather than sprout. With proper moisture, warmth and oxygen, whole wheat or any other seed will begin to grow, in the ground or out. Seventy degrees is ideal. Wheat will germinate at around 40°, but it takes longer to do so in this lower temperature range.

Containers to use. Several types of containers are available. For instance, use

— Containers which have holes in the bottom for drainage; copper wire screen in a frame; metal, perforated sprouting trays; sink strainers or plastic trays with holes punched in the bottom.

— Shallow baking dishes, platters or plates, without drainage facilities.

— Round containers, bottles, crocks or clay pots.

— Rolled, wet towels or wash cloths containing the grain.

Sprouts ready to eat. The sprouts most people are familiar with are the long, white, succulent Chinese variety. Wheat sprouts do not resemble these. Within 24 hours after you begin sprouting, a sprout grows up and three roots grow downward. Eat them when the sprout is the length of the kernel, about ¼ inch long. To obtain a sprout of this length takes about 48 hours, depending on the growing conditions. Eat everything—wheat, sprouts and roots. To retard further growth, refrigerate when the sprouts are at their peak condition for eating. (Wheat sprouts may have a peculiar taste if allowed to grow an inch long, by which time a second shaft and a fourth root will appear.)

#5. SPROUTED WHEAT

I prefer to use one of the following four methods:

Bottle method. Place ¾ cup of clean washed wheat in a quart jar and cover with ¾ cup of warm water. Soak for about 12 hours, drain off the water and drink it (it contains water soluble vitamins and minerals). Rinse the wheat, drain, and put the bottle in a cupboard where it is dark and warm. Don't feel obligated to handle or interfere with germinating wheat. (Like a chicken hatching, it can take care of itself.) Gently sprinkle a little water over the grain two or three times a day (depending on temperature and humidity). There is no need for vigorous washing and rinsing.

Note: For better ventilation, as the sprouts grow tip the bottle on its side. If desired, cover the top of the bottle with a piece of nylon stocking or gauze secured with a rubber band.

Shallow dish method. Cover the bottom of a shallow baking dish with ¼ inch of wheat which has been soaked as in the bottle method. Cover with a wet turkish towel folded to fit the dish. Keep the towel wet, but don't let the wheat stand in water at any time.

Plate and wick method. (This requires no attention for 48 hours.) Cover a plate with terry cloth and sprinkle it with wheat (not soaked) so that the kernels touch each other. Rest the plate on a shallow pan containing water, and have one end of the terry cloth hanging down into the water. (Alternatively, have a separate strip of cloth connecting the water with the terry cloth.) The cloth will act as a wick and draw up water to keep the wheat moist.

Screen frame method. (Twelve inches square is a convenient size for the screen frame.) Over the copper wire put a wet washcloth and cover this with ½ cup of wheat soaked as in the bottle method. Cover the wheat with one or more wet cloths and keep them damp.

Racks and drawers can be made to hold three or four frames. When spraying, take them to the sink and spray from the top with warm water in one dousing. After a moment's draining, put the trays back in place.

Suggestions on Sprouting

My guess is that 99 percent of sprouting failures are due to incorrect amount of moisture. Temperatures and humidity vary so widely that it is almost impossible to give specific instructions on how much moisture sprouts need.

A comparison of an outdoor vegetable garden with an indoor "sprout garden" helps us to understand the process.

Moisture. At first, dry seeds need an abundance of moisture to swell the seeds and soften the outer covering so the sprout and roots can break through. After this happens they are at the mercy of those taking care of them to provide a constant, even supply of moisture.

Some gardeners use the overhead sprinkling method while others sub-irrigate. So it is with sprouting. We can either spray a fine mist of water over the top of the sprout garden or get the moisture to the grain by using wet cloths. The grain can be *under* the wet cloth, *on top* of it, or *in between* wet cloths. Germinating seeds aren't particular about the source as long as they get their moisture.

Temperature and humidity. On a hot, dry day young sprouts may need sprinkling several times to prevent them from withering up and dying. Obviously the moisture requirements will differ from this in a humid atmosphere, or on cool days.

Good drainage. Garden vegetables don't grow submerged in water. Neither do sprouting seeds. Nature causes seeds to make their spurt of growth when water is to some degree withheld. We make sure the soil we plant our garden in is well drained. The same precautions are necessary in sprouting.

Increasing the yield. If food were very scarce, one would want to stimulate the root growth of wheat sprouts to make more bulk. A good way to do this is to make a "wheat mat" by spreading the soaked kernels over a layer or two of cheese cloth on a flat tray. The emerging roots can easily penetrate through and cling on to the cloth. The roots covered with fine root "hairs" (at first resembling mold) stand like legs supporting the wheat kernel.

After the sprouts appear you can provide a humid greenhouse atmosphere by opening a plastic bag on one side and putting it tent-fashion over the tray of sprouts. The roots form a solid mat on the underside of the gauze, which can be held up by two ends without the grain falling off.

Green sprouts. Sprouts turn green in a few hours when exposed to the sunlight, which adds chlorophyll.

Suggested ways to use sprouts in meal planning. Use wheat sprouts in recipes #18, 22, 31, 34, 35, 42, 48, 59, 76, 94, 98, 99, 100, and 101. They are also good in scrambled eggs and omelets, on sandwiches, in casseroles, or sauted lightly in butter.

Growing Wheat Grass

#6. WHEAT GRASS

Spread earth 1½ inches deep in a container and thoroughly wet it. Spread the surface of the earth with wheat which has been soaked for 12 hours (approximately ⅓ cup of wheat for every square foot of earth). Kernels should touch. Cover wheat with ¼ inch of fine soil. Put a wet towel over the top of the soil and keep it moist. After three days, remove the towel and sprinkle the earth gently with water. Keep the earth moist until you cut the grass.

The best environment for growth is a warm, light room, away from direct sunlight. Seven days from planting time the wheat will be about 4 inches high. Cut and use when 4 to 7 inches high. Harvest the crop by cutting close to the soil with scissors. Grind the grass in a meat grinder. Drink 2 ounces of the juice daily, or use the finely-chopped grass in a soup.

After the harvest, break up the sod and allow it to disintegrate in a clean garbage can. It can be used for future plantings. The decayed roots may be used as organic fertilizer.

WILD YEAST AND SOURDOUGH BREAD

#7. WILD YEAST

2 cups flour   2 tsp. honey

2 cups warm water

Mix well and place in bottle or crock, uncovered. Allow mixture to ferment five days in a warm room. Stir it several times a day, thus aerating the batter and permitting the air to activate the mixture. It will smell yeasty, and small bubbles will come to the top.

Wild yeast is used in varying amounts in recipes for bread, rolls, hot cakes, etc. The fifth day after using some, "feed" the starter (to replace the amount used in baking) using equal parts of flour and water or potato water. In another 24 hours the yeast will foam and work and be ready for use again.

Store the unused portion of the yeast in a refrigerator in a glass or crockery container with a tight-fitting lid. Shake it often. To activate it before using it again, add 2 or 3 tablespoons of flour and the same amount of water and stir.

Some say that the yeast spores around the crusty top of the container are beneficial and that one should not keep emptying and washing it.

Variation:

For liquid yeast, peel and cube 3 medium-size potatoes and simmer until tender in 1¼ cups of boiling water. Mix in blender, adding ¼ cup honey, 1½ tbsp. salt and enough cold water to make 3¼ cups liquid. Cool to lukewarm, then add 1 tbsp. dry yeast dissolved in 1 cup lukewarm water. Allow to stand overnight, stir, then use in any recipe calling for yeast.

Always reserve 1 cup as a starter for next baking. Use it in place of the 1 tbsp. of dry yeast needed to get your start going.

#8. SOURDOUGH BREAD

1 cup starter (wild yeast) #7   2 tsp. salt

2 cups warm water   2 tbs. dry milk

3½ cups flour   1 tbs. honey

Mix well, place ball of soft dough in a nest of flour. Knead in only enough flour to keep mixture from sticking. Develop the gluten for 10 minutes by kneading or pounding. Place the satin-smooth ball in a warm bowl and cover bowl with a hot, damp towel. Allow dough to rise for about 5 hours at room temperature (72°) or until it doubles in bulk. (Five hours rising time is characteristic of sour-dough bread made with wild yeast, which takes longer to rise than commercial yeast.)

Shape into 3 loaves and allow to rise again for about 3 hours (use small pans 3½ inches x 7½ inches). Bake at 325° for about 1 hour in a greased or well-floured pan or in juice cans.

BATTER AND DOUGH (UNLEAVENED)

#9. THIN BATTER

2 cups flour   1 tsp. salt

2 cups water (or more)

Mix lightly with *spoon* until free from lumps. Beware of over-beating. Use a squirt bottle or pour direct onto a cookie sheet. Batter makes crisp, tissue-thin snacks, cereals and novelties.

Using squirt bottle. Cut hole in tip just large enough so batter will come through. (Strain batter if it is lumpy.) With this "flowing pencil" create designs on a cookie sheet. Make large and small circles, people, animals, and fruit. Bake at 400° until crisp and brown.

Pouring onto cookie sheet. Use ½ cup dough on a 12-inch x 15-inch cookie sheet. Tip sheet back and forth to cover entire surface. Drain excess off one corner (about ¼ cup) leaving a thin film. For making shapes (as in chapter 8) bake at 375° for about 15 minutes; then peel dough off the cookie sheet before it is completely dried out, shape it and return it to the oven.

#10. THICK DOUGH (to spread)

1¾ cups flour   ½ tsp. salt

1 cup water

Mix lightly with a spoon. For a substantial, crisp, cracker-like bread, spread the rough dough ⅛-inch thick on a cookie sheet. Bake at 350° until brown (about 45 minutes).

#11. STIFF DOUGH (to roll)

1¾ cup flour (plus 2 cups)   ½ tsp. salt

1 cup water

Put thick dough as in recipe #10 in a nest of flour. Knead to a stiff ball (using about 2 more cups of flour). Roll dough out in paper-thin sheets cut in thin strips, or twist and roll dough as fine as string. Bake at 350° until brown (about 45 minutes).

GLUTEN

Gluten is a meat substitute that can be made at home from wheat. Used in various main course recipes it makes emergency meals more appetizing. It doesn't take long to learn how to make it, and then comes the fun of experimenting with recipes, trying to make it taste more like meat. If meat and cheese are scarce, use them in very small amounts as flavoring for gluten dishes.

What is gluten? The wheat kernel contains starch and protein, which can be separated after the wheat has been ground to fine flour. Gluten comes from the protein part of the wheat, and consists of amino acids essential for construction and repair of the body cells. It is insoluble in water and is a tough, elastic substance containing long bands or shreds. Here is a comparison of protein in wheat and meat:

100 gm. of whole wheat   =   560 mg. of essential amino acids

100 gm. of wheat gluten = 3,300 mg. of essential amino acids

100 gm. of beef   = 1,220 mg. of essential amino acids

As explained in chapter 2, any superiority of meat protein over wheat protein would normally be compensated for by the greater amount of wheat in the diet.

How do we serve gluten? There are many ways to serve gluten. For example, serve it in slices as thin as chipped beef. Serve it as you would serve roast beef, sausages or hamburger. For a stew, cut it in cubes after baking it. Grind it for meat loaf. Drop it in soup as you would dumplings. Simmer it to a soft gruel for the baby or the invalid.

How to Make Gluten

#12. GLUTEN

7 cups flour (approximately)   2 cups cold water

Knead into a ball, then follow these three steps:

Develop. Knead, beat, pound or stretch the ball of dough for 10 minutes. Treat it rough! The gliadin and glutenin in the flour must be combined by physical means to develop proper rubber-like gluten.

Wash. To separate the water-soluble starch from the gluten, first cover the ball of dough with cold water and let it stand for about an hour. Then run hot water from the faucet over the dough in a small strainer and catch the water. Work the dough with your hands in the water, washing out the milky starch. As the water becomes milky, pour it off and save it. Keep adding fresh water and working the dough until the water you pour off is clear.

Cook. After the washing process you will have about 1½ cups[1] of raw gluten and will have used a gallon of water or more. (Save the milky water.) Drain the gluten well and knead into a smooth ball. Try cooking the gluten in a variety of ways. Some suggestions follow.

a) Roll or stretch paper-thin and bake on a cookie sheet until nicely brown; cool and cut in meat-like pieces and simmer in salted water for 1 to 3 hours.

b) For small "sausages," roll and cut in 2½-inch lengths, bake until brown, cool, and simmer as above.

c) Press dough one inch thick in small loaf pan, bake at 350° for about an hour, and slice about ⅛ inch thick, or cut in ½-inch cubes for stew.

d) For round slices, bake in small juice cans at 350° for about 1½ hours. Gluten is done when baked through like bread.

e) Drop several teaspoons of raw gluten (before all the starch is washed out) in boiling salted water and simmer for one hour or longer. (These small dumplings will expand, so don't overcrowd them in the pan.)

f) For mush or gruel, first make a fine meal from gluten that has been dried out in the oven. Crush the gluten with a rolling pin

---

[1]Some recipes in this book call for gluten before the starch is washed out, when about four cups of gluten remain.

Water, Flour, and Ball of Dough Soaking

Washing Starch Out of Dough

Foreground: Gluten, Raw and Cooked
Background: Starch Water, and Heavy Starch Washed from Gluten

or grind in a grinder till it has the consistency of corn meal. Stir ⅓ cup of this gluten meal into a cup of boiling water with ¼ tsp. salt. Cook until thick. Use milk or cream instead of water, if desired.

g) Make small round hors d'oeuvres by rolling the dough ½ inch thick and cut with melon ball cutter. Roll to marble size, bake at 350° for about 30 minutes, then simmer in salted water. Insert toothpicks and serve.

Some Questions and Answers About Gluten

Q. How long does it take to develop the gluten?

A. About 10 minutes. You can let a youngster pound it with his fists. I use a big hammer or sturdy rolling pin, or sometimes the blender. I combine half the flour with the water, blending a small amount at a time, and knead in the remaining flour.

Q. After the gluten has been baked, why go to the trouble of simmering it?

A. For two reasons: (a) Moist gluten tastes more like meat and less like bread. (b) Moisture softens the fiber. (Gluten is 57.37 percent fiber, 35.97 percent protein and 4.94 percent fat.)

Q. What kind of wheat produces the best quality gluten?

A. Hard wheat. Gluten from hard wheat is firmer, more elastic, tougher, and darker in color than that from soft wheat.

Q. What other factors assure good gluten?

A. Letting the dough stand in water for an hour or more, and using unsoftened water to wash out the starch, can increase the amount of gluten by as much as 6 percent. (Soft water dissolves the gliadin in gluten.) In summary, you will have proper gluten if you use high protein wheat, physically unite the gliadin and glutenin, use hard water, and wash out the starch in water as hot as the hands can stand. Some people use bags made of loose muslin to hold the gluten as they wash out the starch. I prefer putting one-fourth of the gluten at a time in a fine strainer over a large pan and letting the hot water from the faucet run through it as I work it with my hands.

Q. What do you do with the milky water obtained from washing the gluten?

A. On this emergency diet nothing should be wasted. This water can profitably be used in place of clear water when mixing dry milk, or when making toastum drink, egg nogs, banana drinks, frozen fruit ices, etc. As a food it is a filler, so thicken it or thin it and use it in gravies, soups, sauces and desserts. Use it to starch your clothes or paper your walls. Rub it on your hands to make them smooth and soft, or put it in the baby's bath. Have fun with it—make some paste, or make finger paint with it. Pour it on the soil to nourish your roses or your growing vegetables. Even mop the floor with it — it is a good substitute for floor wax. I have tried all these uses successfully. Whatever else, never throw the gluten water down the drain.

#13. MILK STRETCHER

1 qt. milky gluten water
    before it settles

½ cup dry milk

2 tsp. honey

½ tsp. salt

A few drops of lemon
    juice, if available

Mix and heat to boiling stage in double boiler to decrease starchy taste. Chill. For fresher flavor try pouring back and forth in pans. (It is difficult to distinguish milk stretcher from regular dry skim milk.)

#14. COOKED STARCH (made from milky gluten water)

a) *Very thick.* Leave the milky gluten water for the starch to settle to the bottom. Pour off the clear top liquid and cook the thicker starch to a heavy consistency. Use this as a base for puddings, gravies, cream soups, cereals, pop-overs, etc. (The starch cells burst with very little cooking, forming a heavy batter that leaves the sides of the pan when stirred. It is used in several of the recipes in this book.)

b) *Medium thick.* Combine some of the clear liquid with the thicker white starch that settles to the bottom. Stir constantly while cooking. Use for soups, etc.

MILK-AND-HONEY SWEET BASE

#15. DELICATE DESSERTS — CANDIES

1½ cup non-instant[2]   ½ cup warm honey
    dry milk

Stir and knead enough dry milk into the honey to make a very firm ball. This can be rolled paper-thin, molded and shaped for crafts. For variety, try adding peanut butter; substitute molasses for the honey; add nuts, dried fruit, flavorings and coloring.

BAKING BREAD[3]

Young mother, in baking bread have you ever wondered why sometimes the loaves were high, round and light, and at other times pitifully flat? why a dough that was bouncy and fun to knead gets wet and sticky? why there's a hole through the middle of the loaf, or why the top comes off? why the loaf is so crumbly you can't spread the butter on it? A capsule course in why bread rises and falls may prevent many failures.

Breadmaking Hints

Consistency of bread dough. In stipulating the amount of flour to be used in making bread, many recipes add the words "more or less." The reason is that some flours absorb more moisture than others. The finer the flour, the more moisture required. More flour is needed when water is used instead of milk. In making 100 percent whole wheat bread use as little flour as possible in relation to the liquid used, in order to produce a large-volume, plump loaf.

A good way to insure that the dough is of the proper consistency is as follows. When first mixing the bread, reserve a few cups of the flour and make a nest of it on the breadboard. Pour out about 2 cups of dough in the nest and lift the soft dough from the outside to the center until the dough ceases to stick to the board or hands. Put this ball aside and repeat until

---

[2]The crystal instant milk is granular when mixed with the honey.

[3]Many of these ideas are taken from the book by Rosenvall, Miller and Flack, *Wheat for Man—Why and How*, published by Bookcraft, Inc., 1848 West 2300 South, Salt Lake City, Utah. This is the most complete book I know of on the use of whole wheat flour.

all the dough is used up. Combine the balls of dough, adding the smallest amount of flour possible, then knead or pound to develop the gluten.

Additional ingredients. As a substitute for milk, use warm water, buttermilk, gluten water or whey. For additional ingredients

— Add onions, potatoes, or left-overs of vegetables or cracked wheat cereal.

— Add cheese, nuts, eggs or meat in bread recipes.

— Add extra dry milk, rice polishings, sprouts, wheat germ, or bran.

— Add berries, bananas, currants and raisins, or molasses, for extra calcium and iron.

— Try combining grains — wheat, rye, barley, etc.

— Add to the flour pollen from edible plants.

Generally, any additional ingredients should be added after the first rising, and before shaping the dough into loaves. Note that an overload of other materials in proportion to the gluten may weaken the gluten walls. A stiffer dough is required when other products replace part of the flour.

Bread rising. Bread rising makes me think of blowing a pan of soap bubbles. Growing yeast plants in the dough release moist carbon dioxide gas bubbles. These are encased in a framework made from the gluten in the flour, which is strong, rubbery and elastic, and insoluble in water. These gluten walls stretch, restretch and expand to hold the gas until heat fixes the aerated state of the dough and the result is a high, plump loaf.

In using yeasts, remember that

— You should dissolve dry yeast in water at 110° to 115° (this will feel quite warm to the wrist).

— Soft wheat flour rises more rapidly than hard wheat flour.

— Cold retards the action of yeast. Use cool liquid if you don't want the dough to rise too fast. To delay rising, refrigerate the dough to suit your schedule.

— You can use homemade liquid yeast or wild yeast (recipe #7) in replacement for all or part of the commercial yeast called for in a recipe.

— You can make bread without any yeast if you allow twenty-four hours for rising.

— Butter inhibits the action of yeast, and to a variable extent. Peanut oil or corn oil is better.

— Mineral salts in hard water speed the multiplication of the yeast cells.

— In higher altitudes you may need less yeast or a shorter rising period.

— You can produce yeast by putting a chip from a live oak tree into a mixture of flour and water.

A humid greenhouse atmosphere is conducive to yeast plant growth, and 80° to 95° in a draft-free location is ideal. Temperature of 145° or above will kill the yeast.

The yeasty dough is not at all particular how you warm it up. For instance, you can warm it

— Under the bed covers at camp.

— In the sun.

— In a warming oven.

— Near a radiator or a furnace vent.

— In a bowl set in a deep pan of warm water (90°).

— In an unheated oven with a large pan of hot water below the dough.

— By covering it with a warm damp cloth, warm plate or lid.

— By wrapping it in a blanket or, in winter, red flannels!

— By warming the flour, mixing bowl and baking pans.

When has the dough risen sufficiently? On the first rising when the bread is about double its original bulk press two fingers into the dough. If it holds the indentation and doesn't spring back, it's ready for shaping into loaves.

As a test of readiness for baking, when the loaves look twice as big as they were at first, press one finger lightly and quickly about half an inch into the loaf. If it leaves a little indentation the bread has risen enough (the gluten walls have expanded to the maximum without rupturing). If the finger sinks very quickly into the dough it has risen too much and should be remolded. If the dough remains firm, showing no dent, allow it to rise more (because the gluten walls are still stretching).

Kneading. What we want in the bread is thousands of tiny uniform spaces. Proper punching, kneading and slapping breaks up big gas spaces into small ones. (Gas bubbles are formed by unicellular yeast plants as they divide and ferment.) As we have learned from the section on gluten, for a smooth, elastic dough you must develop the gluten by kneading for 10 minutes or pounding the dough with a hammer, rock, fists, mallet or rolling pin. Dough made from hard-wheat flour requires more kneading than that made from soft-wheat flour.

Shaping the loaf. Stretch and pat out dough into an oblong shape. Firmly pat out the gas bubbles. Fold right and left sides to the center. Pinch edges together to prevent gas from escaping in the final rising. Roll. Place sealed edge down in the pan.

Baking. At the baking stage

— Bake at an even 325° for about one hour and ten minutes, depending on the size of the loaf.

— A baking temperature of 425° is advisable for dough that is slightly lighter than it should be. Reduce the heat after 15 or 20 minutes. (This quickly crusts the bread over before it has a chance to fall flat.)

— A single pan for each loaf is preferred. Narrow pans are better than wide ones. Pyrex or dark metal makes the crust brown. Round cans half full of dough produce a nice loaf for open-faced sandwiches. Don't overcrowd the oven; leave a space between the pans.

— To tell when the bread is done, tap it with the fingers. A hollow sound indicates that the loaf is baked. It should shrink from the sides of the pan. Test with the finger under the crust on a side of the loaf. It is baked if it springs back and is not soggy.

— Turn the loaves if the oven does not bake evenly.

— When the bread is baked, remove it from the pans and cool it on a rack (so the bottom of the loaf doesn't get wet).

Storage of bread. Store bread

— In a ventilated bread box in a dry cool place.

— Frozen.

— In a plastic bag in the refrigerator.

A whole loaf of bread can be completely dried out in the oven and stored in a tin can. Or bread can be sliced very thin and toasted for storage. (When you come to use it, brush it with butter and sprinkle it with onion or garlic powder. Good!) Painting bread with vinegar will prevent mold.

Miscellaneous hints. If you are producing crumbly bread, it may be that you are letting the loaf rise for too long. If you are getting cracks in the loaf, your dough may have been too stiff, or perhaps you did not let the bread rise sufficiently; or maybe the oven was too hot, and this caused the bread to crust over before it had finished rising. A flat loaf containing depressions indicates that perhaps

— The dough was not stiff enough.

— The oven was not hot enough early in the baking.

— The dough was overlight (the gluten walls expanded too much, ruptured, and let the gas escape as a bursted balloon does).

Here are some other general hints:

— If it is inconvenient for you to shape the bread into loaves when it is ready, push your fist into the center of the dough, punch down, and let the dough rise the second or third time.

— The finest textured, lightest loaf of bread I ever made employed only plain water as the liquid.

— When the loaves are being shaped, using shortening on the bread board instead of flour will produce a soft brown crust. To add a shine to the crust, brush it with beaten egg.

WEIGHTS - MEASURES

tbs.	= tablespoon	1 gm.	= 1000 mg.	3 tsp.	= 1 tbs.
tsp.	= teaspoon	28.3 gm.	= 1 oz.	4 tbs.	= ¼ cup
gm.	= gram	453.5 gm.	= 1 lb.	4 cups	= 1 quart
mg.	= milligram			4 quarts	= 1 gallon

Wheat

2½ cups of wheat equals 1 lb.

It takes 1½ cups of wheat (9 oz.) to make 2½ cups of flour.

1 cup of wheat will make 1 quart of wheat sprouts.

To cook wheat in a double boiler use 1 part wheat to 2 parts water.

In a steamer use less water (2½ cups wheat to 3½ cups water). For cracked wheat use 1 cup wheat to 3 cups water.

Batter and dough

1 measure of flour to 1 measure of liquid makes a pour batter.

2 measures of flour to 1 measure of liquid makes a drop batter.

3 measures of flour to 1 measure of liquid makes a soft dough.

4 measures of flour to 1 measure of liquid makes a stiff dough.

Salt

Use 1 teaspoon of salt to 3 cups of liquid for cereals, soups and gravies.

In breadmaking, use ½ teaspoon of salt to every cup of flour.

Milk

> Use 3 tablespoons of dry skim milk (non-instant) to 1 cup water.
>
> Use ¾ cup dry skim milk (non-instant) to 1 quart water.
>
> Use 1⅓ cups crystal (instant) milk to 1 quart water.

Cooking and Baking Temperatures

If your oven has no temperature control and you don't have a thermometer, try the following tests: (a) If a piece of white paper put in the oven turns dark brown in five minutes and not less, the oven is the right temperature for baking bread. (b) Put ½ teaspoon flour on a square made from a paper bag and place in the oven. For cooking rolls, the oven is hot enough if after five minutes the flour has turned light tan. If it is dark brown, the oven is too hot. If the flour is still white, the oven is not quite hot enough.

For outdoor cooking in a reflector oven, the heat will be about right for baking if you can hold your hand in front of the oven for eight seconds. If you can't keep it there that long, the oven is too hot — longer, and it's too cool.

Slow oven — 250° to 300°	Hot — 400° to 450°
Moderate — 325° to 375°	Very hot — 475° or more

A simple test for 150° is whether the hand can momentarily hold food or the metal oven rack without getting burned.

212° is the boiling point of water at sea level. No matter how hot the fire gets beneath it, the water temperature will not exceed that figure. In his book *Guideposts to Health*, John Tobe says that enzymes are lost if food is heated above 120°. Some put this figure at 140°.

CHAPTER 6

Variations of Survival-Four Recipes

This chapter contains well over a hundred recipes and their variants. It goes almost without saying that wherever wheat or flour is referred to in a recipe, whole wheat or whole wheat flour is intended. Note too that when baking, unless you use teflon ware you will normally need to grease or flour the pan — though for some pans the oil in the wheat germ is sufficient to make greasing unnecessary.

MAIN COURSE DISHES

#16. CHINESE WHEAT ROLL-UPS

½ cup raw gluten

½ cup thick gluten water (cooked)

½ cup water

2 tbs. dry milk

Salt to taste

Mix in blender and spread on two cookie sheets. Bake in moderate oven until almost dried out. Peel from cookie sheets. (If too dry to roll, first steam over hot water to moisten.) Spread additional cooked thick starch (#14a) ½ inch thick on top of cooked dough. Sprinkle with soft, steamed, parched wheat. Cut with scissors in strips 1½ x 3 inches. Roll lengthwise and return to oven to brown. Serve hot.

NOTE: Here the gluten is made with milk and covered with milk. The starch dissolves in milk as in water.

Try this: For a filling, use plain steamed wheat and thick mushroom sauce; or use a taco filling (#35).

#17. GLUTEN BEEF

Gluten ‡12a

Roll thin and bake on a cookie sheet until nicely brown. Cut in meat-like pieces and simmer in salted water one to three hours.

Try this: Add dry onion soup mix to the raw gluten.

#18. CHOW MEIN

Gluten cubes #12c   Stew broth #77
Wheat sprouts #5

Combine and serve over crisp shoe-string noodles made from thin batter #9, using squirt bottle.

#19. CREME GLUTEN A LA EMERGENCY

Gluten #12b   Wheat grass #6
Cream Sauce #70

Form the gluten in marble-size balls. Bake and simmer in stew broth #77. Mince wheat grass grown in soil and cut when 1½ inches high. Add gluten balls and grass to cream sauce and serve immediately.

Variations:
(1) Mix wheat grass in blender, using as small an amount of water as possible. Strain, and add a small amount of the green liquid to the cream sauce. (2) Wrap wheat stems in tiny bundles with noodle strips. Serve in a casserole, covering with cream sauce.

#20. EMERGENCY STEW

Gluten cubes #12c   Mock tater tots #26
Stew broth #77   or noodles #27

Combine and serve hot.

#21. EVERYDAY WHEAT LOAF

1½ cups chopped gluten   ½ cup crumbs ‡57
      (cooked) #12   ½ tsp. salt
½ cup thick starch #14a   Stew broth #77
¼ cup dry milk

Combine gluten, starch, milk, crumbs and salt, and shape into small loaf. Pour stew broth over the top. Bake at 350° for 45 minutes.

#22. GLUTEN SURPRISE BUNDLES

Gluten #12a   Noodles #27
Wheat sprouts #5   Salt

Onto a three-inch square of paper-thin gluten put 1 tbs. filling made from crisp noodle crumbs, chopped cooked gluten, and chopped wheat sprouts combined in equal amounts. Bring the four corners of the gluten together and secure with a toothpick. Simmer in stew broth #77 or hot water until heated through.

#23. GOLDEN PIQUANT CASSEROLE

½ cup thick starch #14a   Cream soup #70
½ cup dry milk

Mix starch and dry milk, then chill overnight. Roll into 1½- x 4-inch roll. Knead in more milk if too sticky. Cut in thick slices ¼ to ⅛ inch thick, using nylon thread or cheese cutter. Bake 15 minutes at 350° until golden brown. Place in casserole and cover with cream soup.

Try this: Add grated cheese before or after baking.

#24. LITTLE WHEAT PIES

Baked pie shell #27 or #9   Cream soup #70
Gluten cubes #12c

Just before serving, fill the shell with hot gluten cubes and cream soup.

#25. MOCK CHICKEN LEGS

Taco filling #35   Colored toothpicks
Crumbs #58

Shape the taco filling into small, 2-inch rolls, larger at one end than the other. Roll in crumbs and insert toothpick in small end of each roll. Heat in casserole and serve.

#26. MOCK TATER TOTS

¼ cup dry milk   ¼ tsp. salt
¼ cup flour   1 cup thick starch #14a

Combine, and drop mixture from a teaspoon onto a cookie sheet. Bake until brown. (Make tater tots miniature size.)

Variations:

(1) Spread the dough out thin for crackers. (2) Omit the flour, spread thin on cookie sheet, bake until crisp, and break up for delicious cereal flakes.

#27. NOODLES AND SPAGHETTI

For noodles:

2 cups flour   ½ cup water
1 cup dry milk

Knead or beat for 10 minutes to develop the gluten. Wash out the starch as for gluten #12, using only 1½ quarts hot water, and save the starchy water. (It is not necessary to soak under water.) Yield: ¾ cup gluten.

After washing out the starch, make a smooth ball of dough out of the rough large curds by blending, kneading, rolling or pounding. Spread the batter evenly on a cookie sheet. Bake for 15 minutes at 300°. Peel off cookie sheet before batter gets crisp. (A teflon sheet is preferred.) Roll up and cut into ¼-inch strips with scissors. Unroll strips and put on cookie sheet, and return to oven for about 15 or 20 minutes until crisp but not brown. Keep them white so they will resemble noodles.

Cook the starchy liquid to thicken it. Add 2 tsp. salt and the crisp noodles. Bring to a boil, simmer in top of double boiler for ½ hour, and serve.

Variation:

Use this batter to make marble-size hors d'oeuvres.

For spaghetti: Use ingredients as above, and add sufficient water to mixture to make it suitable for use with squirt bottle. Make fine strings the length of a cookie sheet. Bake at 350° until crisp (about 15 minutes).

#28. PIGS IN BLANKETS

Gluten #12b   Sourdough bread #8

Shape gluten into long rolls ½ inch in diameter. Cut into 3-inch lengths, to look like sausages. Roll bread dough out in sheet ¼ inch thick. Cut in strips 2 inches wide and long enough to go around the sausage. Wrap strip around the sausage, leaving darker gluten ends extending out ½ inch. Allow dough to rise before baking. Heat, and serve with gravy.

Variation:

For "pronto pups," cover sausage with a thinner batter.

Try this: Add dry onion soup mix to the gluten.

#29. PIN-WHEEL BISCUITS

Taco filling #35   Bread dough #38

When dough is ready for final rising, roll it into a ¼-inch sheet. Spread filling evenly over surface of dough. Roll up like jelly roll and cut in miniature biscuits ½ inch thick. Allow to rise until double in bulk. Bake until brown.

#30. SAUSAGE PIZZA

7 tiny sausages for each   Cracked parched wheat #63
   pizza #12b   Cream soup #70
Bread dough #38

Roll bread dough ½ inch thick. Cut into circles of 5-inch diameter. Bake until done. Before putting them on the pizza, simmer sausages in water with salt or bouillon dissolved in it. (They will be tough if left dry.) Spread the round pizza with cream sauce, arrange five of the sausages in a daisy pattern. Form the center of chopped wheat grass. Cut the two remaining sausages in ¼-inch slices and scatter them around the outer edge of the circle. Form a smaller circle with parched wheat.

#31. SAUSAGE SPROUTS

1 cup wheat sprouts #5   ¼ cup water
½ cup noodle crumbs #27   Fine crumbs #9
¼ cup dry milk

Mix milk and water and heat in double boiler. Add noodle crumbs slowly, and steam until soft. Add chopped sprouts. Shape into small rolls and cover with fine crumbs. Serve immediately.

#32. SCALLOPED WHEAT THINS

Noodle dough #27   Wheat grass #6
Good gravy #72

Fill a squirt bottle with noodle dough. Make potato-chip-size shapes and bake at 350° until lightly browned. Place in small casserole dish and cover with gravy. Sprinkle with chopped wheat grass.

#33. SPAGHETTI AND WHEAT BALLS

Wheatburgers #36   Spaghetti #27
Crumbs #54   Gluten gravy #71

Shape gluten mixture in 1-inch balls and roll them in crumbs. Use noodle dough in squirt bottle to add fine strings, and bake on a cookie sheet until crisp. Combine the balls, spaghetti and gravy.

#34. SPROUT CORNUCOPIA

Thin dough #9   Dry milk powder
Wheat sprouts #5   Great wheat grass #6

Make a miniature cornucopia with thin dough. Bake and fill with sprouts dusted with milk powder. For color, serve on a mat of green wheat grass.

#35. TEMPTING TACOS

½ cup wheat sprouts #5   Salt to taste
½ cup steamed wheat #1   Thin dough #9 or
½ cup cooked gluten #12   noodle dough #27
½ cup fine crumbs #51

Make taco shell 4 inches in diameter from thin dough #9 or noodle dough #27. Hold the crisp shell over steam a few seconds so that it won't break when folded over.

Mix sprouts, steamed wheat, gluten, crumbs and salt, and grind in meat grinder several times, keeping mixture light and loose. Heat, and put one rounded tablespoon in each taco shell.

Try this: Season the taco filling with onion soup mix, or add a few cubes of cheese on top.

#36. WHEATBURGERS

2 cups cooked gluten #12c   1 cup dry milk
1 cup crumbs #61   2 cups water
½ cup darker crumbs #57   Salt to taste

Mix ingredients and grind several times in meat grinder. Make a loose burger pattie. Heat through in baking dish at 350° for about 20 minutes.

#37. WHEAT STICKS
(like fish sticks)

Steamed cracked wheat #3   Fine crumbs #54

Press steamed ground wheat in baking dish, chill, and score in ½-inch x 4-inch slices. Roll in fine crumbs and heat in oven.

BREADS AND CEREALS

Bread and Rolls

#38. BREAD STICKS

6 cups liquid milk	⅓ cup oil
½ cup honey	2 tbs. dry yeast
2 tbs. salt	12 cups flour

Dissolve yeast in ¼ cup warm water and 1 teaspoon honey. Mix with liquid milk, oil and salt, and rest of honey. Stir in about half the flour. Put portions of dough in nest of flour on the board, ¼ of dough at a time. Flour the hands. Using as little flour as possible, shape dough into four round balls that are not sticky.

Combine the four balls and develop gluten for about 10 minutes until the dough is springy, smooth, elastic, and easy to handle. Put the ball of dough smooth side up in a warm, lightly-greased bowl and keep it warm until dough doubles in size.

On bread board roll out dough ½ inch thick. Cut with circular cookie cutter, and snip each circle into two equal pieces with scissors. Roll each of these pieces into an oblong. Dip in egg yolk or canned milk, and roll in sesame seed. Allow to rise until dough again doubles in bulk, then bake at 400° until brown and crisp. Makes about 100 bread sticks.

Variations:

(1) Bread stick dough can be shaped into loaves. Make fancy bread by braiding three ropes of dough; or snip top of loaf with scissors in two rows down length of loaf. Sprinkle with sesame seed. Make raisin bread, or flavor with onion or garlic. (2) Use same dough to make hamburger buns, muffins or sweet rolls. (3) For richer dough and a more tender product add 2 eggs to recipe and increase oil to ⅔ cup and honey to ¾ cup.

#39. CLOVERLEAF SOURDOUGH ROLLS
Use basic sourdough bread recipe #8

Roll ½ inch thick. With miniature cookie cutter make rounds and roll into balls, putting three into each muffin cup. Bake at 350° for about 30 minutes until brown.

Variation:

Make small round biscuits and serve with gravy, or make plain bread and serve with hot or cold milk.

#40. ECONOMY BREAD (3½-hour)
(using yeast but no milk or shortening)

6 cups warm water	2 tbs. salt
2 tbs. dry yeast	18 cups flour (approx.)
½ cup honey	

Dissolve yeast in ¼ cup warm water and 1 tsp. honey. Add remainder of water and honey and the salt. Stir in 12 cups flour (loose, warm, and freshly ground). Put 4 cups flour on mixing board. Put about 2 cups of the soft dough at a time into nest of flour and knead in just enough flour so that dough is not sticky. Repeat this until all dough is absorbed, then put 2 more cups flour on the board and knead all the dough together for 10 minutes. (Develop the gluten by either kneading, pounding, or beating.)

Put dough in lightly greased bowl or pan and set in an unheated oven with large pan of hot water (140°) under dough, and damp hot towel over it. (This provides a humid atmosphere.) In 45 minutes dough should be double in bulk. Divide dough into portions according to pan sizes. (From this amount of dough I made 6 small loaves in 3½-inch by 7½-inch pans, also 12 bread sticks, 8 sweet rolls, and 3 hamburger buns.)

Let dough rise in pans until it doubles in bulk again, then bake at 350° for about 1 hour. This makes a light, good bread.

#41. SOURDOUGH BREAD STICKS

Use basic sourdough bread recipe #8

Roll out dough ½ inch thick. Cut with round cookie cutter. Roll in oblong sticks. Dip in milk and roll in crumbs. Bake 30 to 45 minutes at 350° until brown.

#42. THIN SPROUTED WHEAT BREAD

2 cups sprouted wheat #5	1½ tsp. salt

Combine and grind in hand grinder, blender, or juicer. Spread ⅛ inch thick on cookie sheet. Partially bake below 120° then score in squares. Return to oven and bake below 120° until dried out.

#43. QUICK BREAD

8 cups flour	½ cup honey
3 tbs. dry milk	1 tbs. salt
2½ cups hot water	1½ tbs. yeast

Combine dry milk, water, honey, salt and 4 cups flour, and mix in blender until very smooth. (An egg may be included, if desired.) Dissolve yeast in ¼ cup warm water and add to mixture. Mix in remaining flour and allow to stand for 20 minutes. Shape into loaves and allow to rise until double in bulk. Bake at 350° for 30 minutes, then reduce to 300° and bake for another 35-40 minutes, depending on size of loaf.

#44. SOURDOUGH HOT CAKES

1 cup starter #7	1 tsp. salt
2 cups warm water	2 tbs. dry milk
3 cups flour (approx.)	1 tbs. honey

Mix well, put in large bowl. Cover with damp cloth and allow to stand overnight or until double in bulk. (This batter is good for making hot cakes or waffles. The waffles take longer than usual to bake, but are good.)

#45. WAFFLES
(unleavened)

1 cup flour	1 tbs. dry milk
1 cup water	½ tsp. salt

Mix in blender, then bake in waffle iron. Serve immediately while crisp.

Cereals

For economy plus nutrition use whole grain cereals. Commercially prepared cereal costs ten times as much as whole grain cooked cereal.

#46. CRACKED WHEAT CEREAL
(Vary the shape to please the young)
Use cracked wheat recipe #3

a) Using an ice cream scoop, serve as a cereal ball. Dust with dry milk.

b) Press cooked cereal in a baking dish and chill it. Cut in 1-inch x 3-inch oblongs. Toast on all sides under broiler. Serve with warm honey and milk.

c) Use cookie cutters to cut pressed cold cereal into shapes of a star, heart, bird, gingerbread man, etc. Reheat the cereal shapes in oven.

d) Partially dry out the cooked cereal in the oven. Serve hot.

e) For hot cereal with a roasted flavor, parch cracked wheat (see #63) before cooking as in #3. For a small amount of instant cereal, sift the finer parched flour out of the cracked wheat and stir into the boiling salted water.

#47. ROLLED WHEAT

2 cups steamed wheat #1

Roll thin with rolling pin. Bake at 350° until partially dried out. Serve hot or cold.

#48. WHITE MAGIC SPROUTS

Wheat sprouts (48-hour) #5   Dry milk (non-instant)

For a breakfast cereal, sprinkle dry milk over the sprouts and serve immediately with liquid milk and honey.

Try this: Add sliced bananas and coconut, or nuts and raisins.

#49. CEREALS WITHOUT BOXTOPS

(Make cereals at home to resemble the snap, crackle and pop variety you buy in the store.)

Use thin dough #9. Fill a plastic squirt bottle and have fun making different designs on a cookie sheet. Bake at 400° for about 10 minutes until cereals are brown and crisp.

#50. WHEAT FLAKES

Use thin batter #9

Spread ½ cup on cookie sheet and bake at 350° for 15 minutes. Break up big sheets into bite-size pieces.

#51. BREAKFAST FLAKES

½ cup raw gluten #12   ½ cup water
½ cup thick cooked   2 tbs. dry milk
     starch #14

Mix in blender. Either pour onto two cookie sheets and cut into bite-size pieces, or make fancy shapes using a plastic squirt bottle. Bake at 375° for about 15 minutes until crisp.

#52. DIAGONAL PUFFS

Use stiff dough recipe #11. Roll thin. Cut in long, 1/4-inch-wide strips, then cut diagonally in bite-size pieces. Bake at 350° for about 10 minutes until crisp.

#53. WHEAT NUTS BREAKFAST CEREAL

3 cups bread dough #43   3/4 cup honey

Mix, knead, and roll thin. Bake on cookie sheet until hard and dark brown. Break up and grind in meat grinder with medium blade. Serve with cold milk.

Crumbs

On this diet there must be no waste. (Even burned wheat products can be ground and used to make wheat tea.) Any leftovers should be dried out and rolled into crumbs. The reclaimed product can change the appearance of many foods. For different textures and flavors of crumbs try the following:

#54. BREAD (sourdough bread #8 or economy bread #40)

Slice, toast, and grind.

#55. CRACKED WHEAT (#3)

Toast in oven, roll fine.

#56. GLUTEN (#12)

Slice thin, dry in oven, and grind.

#57. PARCHED WHEAT (#63)

Grind coarse or fine.

#58. ROLLED WHEAT (#47)

Roll cooked wheat with rolling pin. Dry flakes out in oven.

#59. SPROUTED WHEAT (#5)

Toast in oven, grind fine.

#60. SWEET CRUMBS (#93)

For crumbs used in pin-wheel cookies.

#61. THIN DOUGHS

Use either flour and water #9, starch #14a or b, or gluten #12. Bake until crisp, and crush in paper bag.

CRACKERS AND SNACKS

Snacks have a place in an emergency diet. Oral gratification serves well to decrease tensions and reduce anxiety and to compensate for frustrations and a sense of dissatisfaction with one's lot.

#62. MOCK WALNUT MEATS

Toasted wheat flakes (#64) resemble walnut halves. Press them in a piece of candy, or use them on ice cream or pudding.

Try this: Add walnut flavoring to melted butter and stir in the hot, dry wheat flakes.

#63. PARCHED WHEAT KERNELS

Method no. 1. Put a layer of plain whole dry wheat in a corn popper or pan and shake on top of the burner until some of the kernels pop and are golden brown. Add salt. You can also parch cracked wheat with fine flour sifted out.

Method no. 2. Spread a layer of steamed cooked wheat on a cookie sheet so the kernels touch each other. Add salt and place under broiler for about 10 minutes until you hear tiny popping sounds. Leave in oven at 250° for 30 minutes longer or until brown and crunchy.

#64. TOASTED WHEAT FLAKES

Grind steamed wheat through a meat grinder using medium blade. Place the flakes on a cookie sheet as they come out of the grinder. Bake until crisp for about 45 minutes at 350°. Add salt and serve.

#65. WHEAT NUTS

Cook thick gluten water in a pan. Stir constantly until it forms a thick, dumpling-like dough. Chill. Run through meat grinder.

Lift the little inch-long curls from the grinder as they come out, and bake on cookie sheets at 350° for about 30 minutes until crisp. They taste like cashew nuts.

#66. WHEAT RINGS

Fill squirt bottle with thin dough #9. Make elongated circles on cookie sheet (they fit the mouth better). Be sure they are tissue-thin. Bake until crisp.

Try this: Add onion powder to the batter for delicious results.

#67. WHEAT THINS

Use recipe #11, #26, or #9. Roll the dough paper-thin, then cut any shapes—round, square, or oblong. Sprinkle with parched wheat crumbs #57 or sesame seeds, glaze with milk, then bake at 375° for 15 minutes until crisp.

DRINKS AND SOUPS

#68. AMBER TEA

Use cookie recipe #89

Continue baking amber cookies until they are dark brown. Reduce cookies to powder-fine crumbs. (Use a blender or roll in a paper sack with a rolling pin.) Pour a cup of boiling water over 1 tbs. of these granules. Simmer for 10 minutes. Strain, and sweeten if desired.

#69. CLEAR SOUP (or beverage)

Toast sprouted wheat in oven until dark brown. Mix in blender until powder-fine. Use about 1 tbs. or less to cup of hot water. (Sweeten with honey to taste if used as a drink.)

NOTE: Clear soups can be made by utilizing liquid left over from cooking wheat or from cooking wheat grass in salted water.

#70. CREAM SOUP

2 cups starch #14b   ½ cup dry milk

Combine and cook in top of double boiler until thick. Salt to taste.

#71. GLUTEN CREAM SOUP

2 cups gluten water #12   ½ cup dry milk
(used to cook dumplings   Dumplings #12
in)

Combine the thick gluten water and pieces of the dumplings with the milk. Mix in blender.

#72. GOOD GRAVY

3 cups steamed wheat   ¾ cup dry milk
3 cups water   Salt to taste

Blend until thick and smooth. Strain out the bran (save it for use as suggested below). Heat in double boiler, or stir constantly in an open pan.

Try this: Use the bran (it makes about 1½ cups) for crackers. Sweeten to taste, and bake on cookie sheet.

#73. GREEN DRINK

See #6

Wheat is mild-tasting in any form. Either drink the grass juice straight, as a nutritious drink, or put a small amount in cream soup.

#74. HONEY AND HOT WATER

For a relaxing bedtime drink try hot water sweetened to taste with honey.

#75. MILK, HOT OR COLD

We could survive on just plain milk for a considerable time. Mix ¾ cup regular dry milk with one quart water.

#76. MOCK CHOCOLATE

½ cup parched wheat   1 tbs. amber tea granules
sprouts   (#68)
1 cup water   ½ tsp. honey
3 tbs. dry milk

Mix sprouts and water in blender. Strain. Add dry milk, blend and heat. Add remaining ingredients, and serve.

#77. STEW BROTH

Combine 4 tbs. toastum (#78) and 4 tbs. amber tea granules (#68). Mix to gravy consistency by adding quart of thickened gluten water. This makes a good liquid for stew or soup.

NOTE: A little flavoring would improve the taste. Try bouillon cubes, onion soup mix, or meat soup stock.

#78. TOASTUM DRINK

Parched wheat, crushed fine and simmered in hot water, makes a good and tasty hot drink. Use 2 or 3 teaspoons to a cup of water, simmer, and strain.

Wheat can be parched in one of three ways: (1) Soak whole wheat overnight and then broil in oven until dark brown. (2) Parch steamed whole wheat in the oven until dried out and dark. (3) Parch dry whole wheat in a corn popper or pan on top of stove.

Variation:

To toastum drink made from very dark brown parched kernels, add cream, honey, vanilla, and nutmeg.

DESSERTS, COOKIES AND CANDY

Desserts

#79. CHEESE-LIKE WHEAT CAKE

1 cup raw gluten #12 (before all starch is washed out)	½ cup dry milk 2 tsp. honey

Mix in blender. Spread out in 7-inch glass baking dish and bake for 1¼ hours at 350°. Pour over cake a syrup made from ¼ cup honey and ¼ cup hot water. Return to oven and simmer for about an hour. Slice in small wedges. Serve with custard-like sauce #80(3).

#80. CUSTARD-LIKE PUDDING

2 cups dry milk 3 tbs. clabber milk #109 (or of yogurt)	3 cups lukewarm water 3 tbs. honey

Mix in blender, then pour into custard cups, gelatin molds, small glasses, or pyrex pie dish. Set in pan of hot water, covering it with

tinfoil or lid to prevent top from getting too brown. Bake at 350°
for 35 minutes or until knife inserted comes out clean. Alternatively,
cook pudding in glasses or cups in a steamer on the stove. Dip
molds or glasses in boiling water for an instant to loosen pudding
from mold, and tip upside down on dish.

Variations:

(1) For ice cream, cool the pudding, freeze, run through fine
juicer[1] or blender. (2) For pie, cover with sweet crumbs, cut in
pie-shaped pieces and serve. (3) For custard sauce, use electric
mixer to make a smooth, custard-like sauce.

#81. WHEAT PUDDING

2 cups steamed whole   ½ cup dry milk
    wheat #1   Honey to taste
2 cups water

Mix in blender until smooth. Strain out the bran with a coarse
strainer. (Use this to make cookies.) Bring the thin mixture to
boil in top of double boiler, then cool. Place in refrigerator to thicken.

#82. ICE CREAM

3 cups steamed whole   ¾ cup dry milk
    wheat #1   ⅓ cup honey
3 cups water

Mix in blender until smooth. Strain out the bran and use for
wheat thins #67. Freeze the smooth paste in a tray until solid, then
use a blender or beaters to make soft ice cream.

Enlarge recipe proportionately as necessary. (This recipe makes
about 1½ cups of ice cream.)

#83. SOFT ICE CREAM (Emergency Flavor)

1 cup dry milk   3 tbs. honey
3 cups water

Mix, put in shallow tray, and freeze solid. Break in small chunks
and beat with electric mixer, blender or juicer. Serve in miniature cones made from dough #51.

---

[1] I use a Champion juicer.

#84. CARAMEL SYRUP

Use recipe for honey caramels (#106), up to the point before kneading in the dry milk.

#85. CARAMEL FILLING

1 cup wheat	½ cup dry milk
2 cups water	3 tbs. honey

Mix 2 cups water, ½ cup dry milk and 3 tbs. honey, and steam whole wheat in this mixture, instead of in water, in top of double boiler. When wheat has absorbed all moisture, put mixture through juicer using fine screen, or use any other means to reduce it to smooth consistency.

To ⅓ cup of the thick caramel syrup add ⅓ cup dry milk and 1 tbs. honey. Beat well, spread on cookies, and broil in oven only a few seconds until brown and set. (This icing is not sticky.)

Try this: Serve the wheat as a pudding when it is thick and brown.

#86. HONEY FROSTING

½ cup honey	½ cup dry milk

Bring honey to boil. Put in top of double boiler. Add dry milk and continue cooking. While cooking is in process, beat frosting with electric beaters until fluffy.

#87. MOCHA FILLING

1 cup honey	½ cup dark toastum drink
1 cup dry milk	(made with 1 tbs. toastum #78 to ½ cup water)

Cook over boiling water in double boiler until thick. Use as cookie filling or icing.

#88. WHITE FLUFFY ICING

Spoon off thick foam after making a gallon of powdered milk in blender. Put in bowl, add dry milk, and mix with electric beater. Trickle thin honey into bowl. When fluffy, serve on spoons made of wheat. Eat spoon and all!

Cookies

#89. AMBER TEA COOKIES

1 cup raw gluten #12 (before all starch is washed out)	1 cup very thick cooked starch #14
1 cup dry milk	½ cup honey
	¼ tsp. salt

Mix in blender. Spread thin on cookie sheets. Score into small squares. Bake in moderate oven until crisp.

#90. BARBER POLE STICKS

Bread dough #38   Basic candy #15

Roll out the dough ¼ inch thick. Cut small circles and roll them up into pencil-size-long rolls. Bake until brown, then cool. Roll out candy in same way as the dough, then wrap candy rope around the stick, barber pole style.

#91. CRISS-CROSS COOKIES

1 cup flour	¼ cup honey
¼ cup dry milk	½ tsp. salt
¾ cup water	

Mix and pour in squirt bottle, then make designs on cookie sheet. Bake at about 350° for approximately 15 minutes.

#92. FORTUNE COOKIES

2 cups gluten water #14b	¼ cup honey
½ cup dry milk	

Cook the gluten water to consistency of thick gravy. Mix in blender with milk and honey. Fill squirt bottle and make large dollar-size cookie. Bake at about 350° for about 15 minutes. Put a "fortune" inside and fold over.

#93. HONEY CHEW COOKIES

2 cups gluten water #14a	½ cup honey
½ cup dry milk	½ tsp. salt

Cook the gluten water to a thick mixture. Using an electric beater or blender, combine it with the other ingredients. Fill a squirt bottle and make designs on cookie sheet. Make plain nickel-size circles or try a daisy pattern. Bake at 350° for about 15 minutes.

#94. HONEY DROP COOKIES

½ cup ground sprouted
wheat #5
1 cup flour

½ cup water
1½ tbs. dry milk
4 tbs. honey

Mix well. Drop teaspoons of mixture on cookie sheet and flatten out. Bake 20 minutes at 350°

#95. PETAL CUPS

Use basic recipe #15

Roll thin and cut petals from pattern. Shape three petals over the back of a small muffin tin. Let the air dry them out.

#96. PIN-WHEEL COOKIES

Use basic recipe #15

Roll out in thin sheet and cover with crumbs made from honey chew cookies (#93) crumbled, toasted, and moistened with milk. Roll up and cut with a string into small slices.

#97. RIBBON COOKIES

With thin dough recipe #9 in a squirt bottle, make lines across a cookie sheet ¼ inch apart and bake until set. Remove from oven and fill the spaces with criss-cross cookie recipe (#91). Return to oven to bake lightly, then cut in 3-inch x 1¼-inch wafers. Bake at 350° for about 15 minutes.

#98. SPROUT COOKIES

Basic candy recipe #15   Sprouted wheat

For "sprout bundles": Roll candy mix paper-thin and cut into 1½-inch squares with pinking shears. Place 1 tsp. sprouted wheat in center of each, and pinch two opposite corners together.

For "filled cookies": Put sprouts between two small circles cut from basic candy recipe #15. Press edges together with fork indentations.

#99. SPROUT CRISPS

1½ cups 48-hour sprouted·   2 tbs. honey
    wheat   ¼ cup dry milk
½ cup water   ⅓ cup flour

Mix water and sprouts in blender on low speed. Blend to a mush and add remaining ingredients. Spread tablespoons of batter as circles on cookie sheet. Bake at 300° for 40 minutes. Makes 12 jumbo or 30 small cookies.

#100. TINY THREES

Sprouted wheat   Honey

Grind enough sprouted wheat to make a cup of thick starch. Use a cone-shaped colander to strain the thick, smooth starch.

Mix in 2 tbs. honey. Fill a squirt bottle and fashion nickel-size cookies. Bake at 350° until golden brown. Cool and put together, sandwich style, with ¼ tsp. of caramel filling (#84).

#101. UNBAKED COOKIES

Sprouted wheat   Honey
Cookie crumbs #89

Combine equal parts finely-chopped sprouts and cookie crumbs. Mix in enough honey to hold mixture together. Form into small balls.

#102. WAFERS

Use basic recipe #15

Roll thin and cut in 1-inch x 2-inch strips. Broil for a second until bubbly and brown, then cool.

#103. WHEAT SQUARES

½ cup honey   2 tbs. water
½ cup dry milk   2½ cups cooked wheat

Boil honey about 2 minutes to soft ball stage. Add dry milk and water. While mixture is cooking in top of double boiler, beat with electric beater until fluffy and smooth. Add whole steamed wheat (#1) that has been partially dried out on a cookie sheet in the oven, but is still soft.

Sprouted Beans and Seeds

Six Ways to Use Wheat

Desserts

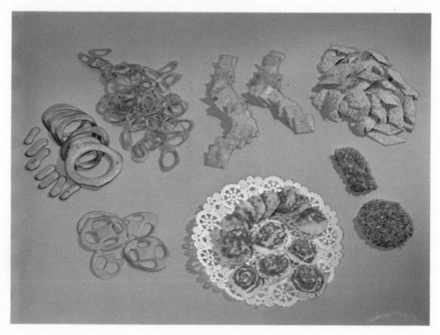

Cookies and Crackers

Wheat Sprouts and Grass

Gluten Dishes

Candies

Chapter 7 Menu — Sunday Dinner

Chapter 7 Menu — Monday Dinner

Chapter 7 Menu — Tuesday Dinner

Chapter 7 Menu — Thursday Dinner

Chapter 7 Menu — Saturday Breakfast

Chapter 7 Menu — Saturday Lunch

Spread mixture an inch thick in shallow pan. Cut in squares and serve immediately. (If this is allowed to stand, the potassium in the honey will draw the moisture out of the wheat, and you will have hard kernels and sticky candy.)

Candy

Don't expect to close your eyes and go off to dreamland while mouth-melting goodies slip down. But these candies have eye and taste appeal, and are good for you.

#104. ALL-DAY SUCKERS

1 cup honey $1\frac{1}{2}$ cups dry milk

Cook honey to hard crack stage[2] at 285°. Remove from heat, and immediately add enough dry milk to make a stiff ball. Smooth out the lumps. Roll into small balls, insert sucker sticks and allow to harden.

Try this: Before shaping into balls, add vanilla or other flavoring or coloring.

#105. BASIC CANDY

Use basic recipe #15

Vary the shape. Roll and cut into pieces the size of pine nuts, small mints, or small oblongs. Or grind pieces of the firm candy in the meat grinder, and as they come through form them in pointed chocolate-drop shape and size or in small circles.

Variations:

(1) Substitute molasses for honey in basic recipe #15. (2) Color candy red or green and use raspberry or mint flavoring. (3) Add peanut butter to basic recipe #15. (4) Use equal parts of soybean flour, dry milk and peanut butter, moisten with lemon juice and honey, and roll out. Mold in pecan-roll shape, and cut in slices with a string. (5) For macaroons, add fine coconut to basic recipe #15. Shape in small balls, flatten with thumb and forefinger, and brown under broiler.

---

[2]To test without a candy thermometer, remove pan from heat, pour small amount of honey from a spoon into a glass of cold water. Candy is done when the sample is hard enough to make a tinkling sound when hit against side of glass.

#106. HONEY CARAMELS

1 cup honey   ½ cup water
1 cup dry milk

Mix until free from lumps. Cook in top of double boiler for 45 minutes, stirring often; or, for a darker caramel color, put pan directly on burner on low heat for a few minutes, and stir vigorously. (Dry milk has a high percentage of milk sugar in it that burns readily, as sugar does when caramelized.) Cool, and knead dry milk into the syrup to desired consistency. Roll in ½-inch roll. Cut pieces one inch long and shape into squares.

#107. HONEY TAFFY

1 cup honey

Cook to hard crack stage at 285°. Stir occasionally. Remove from heat and pour onto buttered platter. As outside edges cool, fold to the center and start stretching while still hot. Pull until light and porous and until small strings develop.

#108. PARTY SWEET TREAT

Use basic recipe #15.

Roll thin, then cut in circles one inch in diameter. Cut in ¼ inch from edge at two opposite points. Press opposite sides together until they meet. (This will look like a fluted pie-crust.) Makes 50.

NOTE: See chapter 8 for more variations to basic candy recipe #15.

COTTAGE CHEESE AND YOGURT

#109. COTTAGE CHEESE (Small Curd)

2 cups dry milk   2 quarts water

Mix in blender, then allow to stand until firm clabber is formed. (This may take 70 hours at room temperature [70°]. At 85° it will take about 50 hours. There is probably a quicker method of getting the milk to clabber but I have not discovered it.)

Add boiling water equal to the amount of clabber. Allow to stand 4 or 5 minutes, then gently pour off excess liquid and strain through cheese cloth or a colander. Add about a gallon of boiling water to the curd and allow to stand until it is set and has body.

Drain, and turn the curd into a bowl. Add salt (and cream, if you have it).

Try this: Make cream cheese by blending the cottage cheese to a smooth consistency. Season, and use as a dip for wheat thins.

Make hard cheese by putting the cottage cheese in cheese cloth under a weight. When moisture is squeezed out, roll out thin slices between waxed paper.

#110. YOGURT

2 cups dry milk   3 cups lukewarm water

Mix and stir well. Add about 3 tbs. clabber milk (or yogurt already made). Pour into warm jar, put in warm oven (80°), and leave there for 2 or 3 hours or until set. Refrigerate immediately.

Survival Menus

Now that we have about one hundred recipes available, let's draw up some sample menus. If you have wheat, dry milk, honey and salt you can serve the meals suggested in this chapter. Additional flavoring is optional, though obviously desirable for taste and variety. Actually, while I have deliberately placed great emphasis on the ability to survive on the four emergency foods, most housewives will see that they have additional foods available for meal preparation, such as flavorings for the gluten (bouillon cubes or dry onion soup mix), cheese for the tacos, mushroom soup for the steamed wheat, and vanilla, cinnamon, colorings, flavorings, coconut, yeast cakes, oil, and butter for desserts and breads.

Remember that the intent of time-consuming preparation of "fancy foods" is to add eye and taste appeal. Small sample-size portions fill that need. Persons with large appetites can "fill up" on plain steamed wheat.

Perhaps your family would like to try what mine did — an experiment over a period, using only the survival foods. Here are menus covering one week. If you feel a little apprehensive about the outcome, give yourself a good start by persuading your family to simulate survival conditions and go on a twenty-four-hour fast—then start serving your survival menu meals with Sunday dinner immediately after the fast!

SUNDAY

Dinner

Wheat rings hors d'oeuvres #66
Chipped gluten beef and gravy
    #17 and #77
Steamed wheat #1
Custard-like pudding #80
Honey chew cookies #93
Wheat grass #6
Toastum drink #78

Supper

Tempting tacos #35
Cream soup #70
Amber tea and cookies #68 and
    #89

Between-meal snacks

Wheat nuts #65 and candy #108
    for grown-ups
All-day suckers #104 for kids

MONDAY

Breakfast
Sourdough hot cakes #44
Caramel syrup #106
Gluten sausage #28
Cold milk

Lunch
Cottage cheese #109
Thin sprouted wheat bread #42
Clear soup #69

Dinner
Green drink #73
Emergency stew #20
Noodles #27
Bread sticks #38
Criss-cross cookies #91

Snacks
Toasted wheat flakes #64

TUESDAY

Breakfast
Cracked wheat oblongs #46
Mock chocolate #76

Lunch
Golden piquant casserole #23
Wheat sprouts #5
Milk

Dinner
Hors d'oeuvres #27

Green cream soup #70 and #73
Thin sticks #9
Wheatburgers #36
Oven-cracked wheat #46d
Soft ice cream #83 with caramel
    syrup #84
Barber pole sticks #90
Cold milk

Snacks
Wheat thins #67

WEDNESDAY

Breakfast
Cold cereal—breakfast
    flakes #51
Sprouts #5
Milk

Lunch
Scalloped wheat thins #32
Custard-like cheese cake #80(2)

Dinner
Cream soup #70
Pigs in blankets #28
Creamed wheat #1
Toastum #78 and a roll #39
Wheat pudding #81

Snacks
Honey taffy #107

THURSDAY

Breakfast
Steamed wheat #1
Toastum #78
Lunch
Sausage sprouts #31
Cream soup #70

Dinner
Sprout crisps #99

Gluten cream soup #71
Pin-wheel cookies #96
Bread #8
Milk

Snacks
Spaghetti #27 and wheat balls #33

FRIDAY

Breakfast

Biscuits and gravy #39 and #72
Chipped gluten beef #17
Milk

Lunch

Little wheat pie #24
Cloverleaf sourdough roll #39

Dinner

Clear soup #69
Chinese wheat roll-ups #16
Sprouts #5
Amber tea #68
Fortune cookies #92

Snacks

Tiny three cookies #100

SATURDAY

Breakfast

Waffles #45
Caramel syrup #84
Green drink #73
Rolled wheat #47
Amber tea #68

Lunch

Sausage pizza #30
Gluten cream soup #71
Milk

Wheat sprouts #48
Candy #105

Dinner

Green drink #73
Everyday wheat loaf #21
Steamed wheat #1
Barber pole stick candy #90
Milk

Snacks

Parched wheat #63

ADVANCED PREPARATION

If you plan menus ahead and do advanced baking and cooking, you can prepare "jiffy" meals even in a survival situation. Also, you can impress the boss who is coming for dinner, or be prepared when friends drop in.

About ten days before trying out the survival menus plant flats of wheat (#6). Six days ahead start the wild yeast (#7). Four days ahead sour the milk for cottage cheese and pudding. (Sour milk can be frozen in cubes to use when needed.)

A day or so ahead
— Make the gluten for several meals, using freshly ground flour.
— Bake rolls, crackers, biscuits, and breakfast flakes.
— Make taco and little wheat pie shells.
— Make wheat rings, snacks, and candy.
— Parch wheat for toastum.
— Bake six kinds of cookies.
— Freeze the ice cream and make caramel syrup.

CHAPTER 8

Just for Fun

The United States has the most liberal food habits in all the world. In stark contrast to the inhabitants of many other nations, where an environment of poverty and deprivation saps the powers of enjoyment, to a great many Americans food is a source not merely of nourishment but of pleasure.

So let's dare to experiment with food. Do it now, *before* any emergency arises. Creativity must be preceded by thought, and who knows how crowded our thoughts might be in circumstances making us dependent on the survival diet! In a time of scarcity, keeping busy and happy under the stimulus of creative activity would help to dull those hunger pangs, and the resulting snacks and other edible "creations" would help us to overlook the missed meal. And in normal circumstances any creative time spent with food is time well spent if it amuses the young, filling their otherwise empty hours, or provides a party treat or a surprise for the bedside tray.

MATERIALS FOR CREATIVE FUN

Many people have learned to be creative with familiar materials like icing in a pastry tube, or with paper, yarn, pipe cleaners, etc. If we will give vent to our inventive genius we can learn just as well to create with flour, water, salt, milk, and honey. The equipment and supplies for this are all around us, as the next few paragraphs suggest.

Electrical equipment. Most American kitchens have stoves with knobs which regulate heat from simmer to hot and ovens that broil or bake as desired. We have refrigerators and freezers and electric mixers, blenders, choppers, grinders and juicers.

Kitchen drawer and shelf. The kitchen contains a rolling pin, spatula and pancake turner, potato masher, cookie cutter, cheese and egg cutters, a wire egg beater and a melon ball spoon. It has plain and colored toothpicks, plastic bottles, tin dishes, and rolls of colored foil.

Desk drawer and sewing room. Here we find a ruler, plastic triangle, paper punch, penknife, scissors, pinking shears, needle and thread, thimble, buttonhole cutter, and a tracing wheel we can use for scoring.

Craft books. From craft books you can trace patterns for snow flakes, paper dolls, birds, trees, a butterfly, or holiday symbols. Use patterns for such things as a flower, basket, windmill, fan, tent, or turkey.

Unconventional baking and serving. For producing "different" shapes use the back of small muffin pans, metal ice cube dividers, wooden ice cream sticks or spoons; or bake strips of dough around tin cans, from frozen juice size to gallon size. For serving on special occasions, try using snack dishes, trays and platters which, while not of crystal and gold, are precious and old and therefore harmonize with man's ancient foods which are to be served on them. And for "brisk" sales, package attractively — save your chocolate boxes; use lace doilies, paper plates and napkins of delicate color, bordered paper towels, or kitchen wraps.

Suggestions for Creative Fun

There is no miracle about being creative with our basic foods. By using your growing collection of tricks of the trade, including items such as I have suggested above, you can surprise and delight both family and friends as well as gratify some of your own creative urges. Some suggestions follow.

Fun with Dough

Dough as fine as string. Use recipe #11. Roll out on a floured board. Cut ½-inch strips with a ruler. Twist to get the roll started, then press down with the palm of your hand as you roll. With this you can make things like

— Picture frame, any size, made by braiding the dough. Try an oval one, with a tiny bow at the bottom. (The picture inside could be an arrangement of rose buds made from #15.)

— House. Make wheat sticks the size of matches and place alternately, log cabin style.

— Flower pot. Using honey for glue, on colored paper place small wheat sticks to form a flat flower pot, with a daisy in the center.

— Spirals. Wind string dough around ice cream sticks, bake, and remove carefully.

— Running stick men. These are fun to make from matchstick-size dough.

— Miscellaneous. Write your name, weave a mat, make flower stems or geometric border designs.

Paper-thin dough. Use cookie cutters, or cut around heavy paper patterns with a sharp knife, and bake until crisp. You can make

— Star necklace. Bake star cookies with a pencil-size hole in the middle. String several of them on a white candy rope (#15).

— Funny face. Cut out the eyes, nose and mouth. Make bushy eyebrows from wheat grass.

— Tasty spoons. Use these to eat ice cream.

— Brown cow. Have it graze in a miniature green wheat field.

— Butterfly or bird. Cut from a pattern.

— Tent with an open door and a wheat-stick camp fire in front of it.

— Fan, for a hot day — folded like a paper one.

— Flower basket, cone shaped, scalloped on top, with paper-punch designs.

Strips of dough. Dough strips are another possibility for just-for-fun things. With them make

— A chain, either with tiny links, or with big ones for the Christmas tree.

— A "weave" mat for a vase of flowers.

— Spiral strips, baked around small and large cans. (Bake, and remove gently.) Hang by a string for springy fun.

— Clothes pins. Strips folded over the edge of a can and baked.

— A zig-zag fence made from a 1-inch strip strung up and down over metal ice cube dividers.

Speedy dough art. Have fun with dough in a plastic squeeze bottle. Anything you can draw with crayon or chalk you can make with this "flowing pencil." Use #9 to

— Make a man in the moon, an ice cream cone, a boy or girl.

— Draw some stockings, spectacles, a hat, or a house.

— Write your name, or make a tic-tac-toe game, a wagon or a train.

— Make a teacup with a handle.

— Draw lines on a cookie sheet back and forth, basket-weave style, for a place mat.

— Make a crown for your young one's head, a charm brace-let, or rings for the fingers.

Spring Flower Show

Throughout history artificial flowers have been made from countless materials. Why not from wheat, honey, milk and salt? Try making

— Calla lillies. Roll out a thin sheet of white candy #15. From a pattern, cut and shape a lily and form it around a stamen (a wheat stick soaked in honey and baked until dark brown). Make a leaf and a bud, arrange them on the stem, and place the entire creation flat on a latticed-wheat wall hanging.

—Cattails. Shape a pencil-size weiner with a point at the top. Make a smaller stem and bake it first. For a brown color, soak the top in honey and bake, wrapping the lower part of the stem in the tin foil so that it won't get brown.

— Daisies. Make a white one cut from a pattern. Sprinkle parched wheat in a circle for the center.

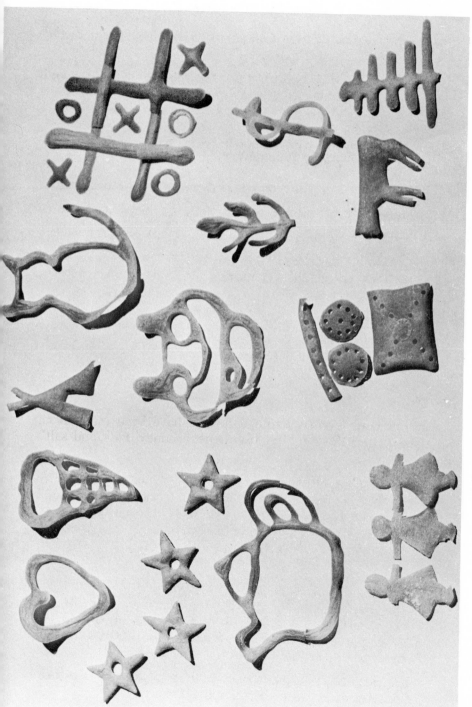

— Spring blossoms. Shape tiny white candy blossoms spiral-fashion up a curved baked wheat stem.

— Wheat carnations. (Originally an accident, like many of my creations.) Consists of thin dough which stuck to the pan, scooped up pleated fashion.

— Wild flowers. Prebake curved stems and stand them in a small can. Slip nickel-size circles of rolled dough over the top of the stems, leaving them about an inch apart on the stem. Return to oven to bake the flowers.

— Wheat roses. (They look like Hawaiian wood roses and are beautiful.) Bake thin dough #9 until it lifts from the pan while the inside is soft and pliable. Cut petals from pattern (steam before cutting if the dough is too crisp). Shape petals around wheat stem, and remove extra dough at point of attachment to stem by soaking with a few drops of hot water so it can be molded smooth. Finish baking by hanging down in oven, or use a heat lamp.

— Maidenhair fern. Made from dough stuck to a teflon cookie sheet after a thin sheet has been peeled off. Return to oven until the gossamer sheet lifts up. Gently arrange it in your rose bouquet.

— Gluten curls. Grind chilled raw gluten in a meat grinder. Bake the curls on a cookie sheet as they come out of the grinder.

Wheat Grass Fun

For fun with wheat grass

— Grow wheat grass in an old shoe, in sea shells, in a tiny egg shell, in a big coconut shell — in anything interesting that holds soil.

— Weave a wheat grass basket and fill it with parched wheat for a party favor.

— Make a grass hula-hula skirt for a doll. (Braid washed roots from 5-inch-tall grass to form the band.)

— Bake a funny cracker face. Add bushy eyebrows made from wheat grass pushed through a narrow slot.

If you get really ambitious make an edible party centerpiece of "home sweet home." To do this

— Grow a flat of wheat 6 inches tall, and make a clearing in the center to nestle a new home.

— From a cardboard pattern, cut out the sections (the way a gingerbread house is made) and bake.

— Assemble your "prefabricated" home with the aid of some masking tape inside.

— Make white candy tie-back curtains.

— Employ a "landscape artist" to curve the walk to the front door and top it with parched wheat.

— Neatly clip the grass lawn, enclose with a picket fence made from thin dough.

— Have roses 'round the door, a bench and a bird bath in the shade of the lawn.

The home is now ready for occupancy. (For a home in the Ozarks, have wash tubs on the side of the house, grandpa cutting wood, long underwear on the lines, and a brown cow in the pasture.)

Sprouting Fun

Wheat will sprout anywhere it can find moisture. To enjoy it visually

— Sprout it in thimble-size paper cups, on butter-pat plates, or in designs formed on colored washcloths.

— Sprout it on wet towels in cookie cutter shapes. Try geometric border designs.

— Sprout it in a jumbo-plate-size daisy-shaped pattern.

— Combine wheat sprouts with alfalfa seed and mung beans. For example, plant one circle inside of another. You will readily think of many other designs.

— Color the sprout roots with berry juice for decorative contrast.

— Grow the sprouts to a maximum of one inch high on cheese cloth. Pick up the cloth with a solid mat of roots on the bottom, and hang it by the window — perhaps on a clothes hanger. Spray often with water. Watch sprouts turn green in a day in the sun. Watch the water droplets at the tip of the blades sparkle like jewels.

Wheat Kernel Crafts

Use wheat kernels the way the Islanders use "brown elephant ear seeds." They make earrings, purses, necklaces, etc., of them. Use wheat, too, the way Indians use sand to make paintings. (Parched wheat can be light brown or dark brown.) For these crafts

— Under a large magnifying glass, thread soaked soft wheat on a fine needle with nylon thread.

— Spread gluten water starch on parts of a picture you want to "paint," then sprinkle various grains and grinds for the desired effect.

— Glue grains in a design on a tiny matchbox for a trinket case.

White Candy Fun

People through the ages have written on silver and gold, copper and tin, wood and leather, papyrus and stone. You can write on a sheet of milk and honey (#15), rolled paper-thin. Boil toastum drink (#78) down for dark ink, dip in a clean straight pen, and write "Dear John . . ." (The ink has a gold sheen to it when dry.) For a bedside tray, roll a miniature letter up in a scroll and tie it with a blue ribbon.

For other fun with this medium

— Make lovely lacy snowflakes from a pattern. Cut with a penknife.

— Make tiny dishes, or a table, chair or bench. Make a bed, a pillow, and put a baby under the covers. Shape a white duck or chicken. Mold a temple (add raised floral designs as on Thailand temples). Make statues and monuments.

Hints and Techniques

Here are some useful hints for creative fun with food.

— Think small! Get used to experimenting with small amounts for small "creations" which intrigue the young and conserve food supply. When you are sure of yourself you can increase the recipe to feed a hungry family.

— Uniformity of rolled products for bread sticks or marbles is best achieved by cutting circles any size desired, then quickly shaping them with the hands.

— For eye appeal of baked wheat products if no oil, egg, or cream is available, dip in or brush on liquid milk. For sweet foods use honey thinned with water.

— Have baby food jars on hand filled with many kinds of crumbs to use in cooking.

— Use a damp sponge to "erase" squirt bottle mistakes on a cookie sheet.

— Shape dough over steam if it is too crisp to cut without breaking, or put sheets of crisp dough between steaming towels. (Shape roses over steam.)

— Interesting effects are obtained by baking in successive steps. For example, first bake flat cookie design petals, then add in-between dots to prevent them from running together.

— Curl rose leaves around a plastic drinking straw.

— Use darning needle or nut pick to make holes.

— Put a weight on a creation in the oven to keep it from curling.

— Thin dough #9 can be handled like fabric. Sew it with needle and thread — make a doll dress, for example.

— Use a springy egg beater to make a design on the back of a dough turtle, and color it with toastum drink for variegated colors.

PART III

OTHER SURVIVAL
TECHNIQUES

CHAPTER 9

Food Preservation

Preserving and storing food is both an art and a science. Those of us who had rural beginnings have the advantage of having some "know-how" in this area. Of necessity, on the farm we preserved food from one harvest season to the next.

Today we don't need to preserve our own food, even for survival, if we have the money to buy it already processed. There are companies which provide, in storage form, moisture-free foods such as steaks, stew, fruit, vegetables, eggs, and desserts, any of which would be a tasty addition to our four survival foods.

But it is still to our profit to know some tricks of the trade in food preservation and storage. With this know-how we can take advantage of food surpluses and bargains. And future circumstances (when perhaps there will be no time for research or experimentation) may materialize in which we will be glad for our experience in freezing, drying, salting and brining, smoking, fermenting, canning, and storing foods. It may make the difference between adequate food and hunger for our families and loved ones.

This chapter, then, deals with methods of preserving food. The next one is concerned with food storage.

HOME FREEZING

Freezing is a safe and easy way to preserve perishable foods, because bacteria can't grow in zero temperatures.

Home freezing is more successful if the packages of unfrozen food are taken to a locker for quick freezing before being stored in one's deep freeze. If this is not practical, be sure to

— Place packages of unfrozen food against the wall surface of your home freezer.

— Space packages apart.

— Keep the new packages away from food that is already frozen.

— Restrict the amount of food you are freezing to no more than 10% of the freezer capacity at any one time.

The reason commercial food packers use the quick-freeze method is interesting: Foods are composed of microscopic cells containing moisture. If food is slow-frozen, this moisture slowly forms large ice crystals that rupture the cells. Because of this rupture, when the food is thawed the juices escape and there is a loss of flavor, nutrients and juiciness. When the food is quick-frozen the cell walls remain firm and unbroken.

Directions for Freezing

String beans (Kentucky Wonder are the best.)

1. Wash whole tender beans and steam them for 3½ minutes, one pound at a time, in a wire basket above 2 inches of boiling water.

2. Chill in cold running water, then in ice water.

3. Pack in any size ordinary canning jar with a two-piece screw top lid (or package in moisture/vapor-proof bag). (Leave ½-inch head space in the bottle.)

4. Place in the freezer.

The method is the same for most vegetables, except that the steam time may vary. Broccoli, for example, needs to be steamed for 5½ minutes.

Greens (Mustard greens, beat greens, turnip greens, Swiss chard.)

1. Wash young tender leaves, discarding thick main stems.

2. Water scald (do not use the steam method). Put a pound of leaves in a wire basket or cheese cloth and immerse in 2 gallons of boiling water for 3 minutes.

3. Chill immediately as for beans, drain and package.

4. Place in the freezer.

When serving them you could mix frozen greens with pineapple juice in a blender for a green drink, or use them in cream soup.

Eggs (Keep from nine months to a year.)

Use only fresh (no off-odor), clean, uncracked, chilled eggs. Yolks and whites can be frozen separately.

1. Stir yolks and whites with fork. (Do not beat.)
2. Package in baby food jars, waxed paper cups, etc. (Allow ½-inch headspace in all containers.)
3. Place in the freezer.

To use frozen eggs, thaw in refrigerator or under cold running water. Use within 24 hours.

Fish

Glazing takes the place of moisture/vapor-proof materials used in wrapping. A thin layer of ice seals the food, preventing air from getting to it. Whole fish, poultry, and game are foods most often glazed. The procedure is simple.

1. Freeze unwrapped.
2. Dip quickly in water which is just above freezing point. The zero temperature of the food will set a thin film of ice over the product.
3. Place in freezer.
4. Repeat the water dip and freeze procedure until glaze is ⅛ inch thick.

Miscellaneous Ideas on Freezing Food

Soft peach ice cream. Odd-shaped pieces of fruit (e.g., peaches) from windfalls, etc., can be frozen in a sweetened custard sauce. When you are ready to use it, break it in chunks and mix in a blender.

Frozen bananas. Peel bananas and freeze them whole. Slice frozen banana in a dessert dish, glaze it with cream and top it with a red cherry and chopped nuts. Serve immediately.

Frozen carrot juice. For a nutritious snack, freeze carrot juice in ice cube trays, first inserting a sucker stick in each cube. As a variation, blend with pineapple juice before freezing.

Frozen baked bread. This keeps for up to a year in zero temperature.

Soup mix. Have a "soup bottle" in the freezer. Add small amounts of left-over vegetables until there is enough to make soup for the family.

DRYING FOOD AT HOME

We marvel at new commercial methods of dehydrating food, but although there is currently a revival of interest in the home drying of foods we find very little written on home drying since World War II, when Victory garden surpluses made this a popular method of food preservation. Certainly in our effort to be self-sustaining we should know about one of the oldest and most natural methods of preserving food.

Advantages of Dried Food

— Nutritive values remain high.

— Dried food occupies only about one-fourth as much space as ordinary canned goods.

— Spoilage and rotation worries are reduced.

— There is no waste.

— New dried foods are helping to alleviate world hunger.

— Food bars, squeeze tubes of food, tablets and juice crystals are new, space-age foods. In trips to the moon and back, weight and storage space are important factors. So they are also in mobile home living and in today's compact apartments and homes.

— Should you change homes, dried foods are easily transported.

— They are ideal for travelers, hikers, campers, rescue workers, etc. (Instead of carrying 16 fresh apricots with you, carry a pound of dried ones — 175 of them.

Dehydrator

The Drying Process

Many apparently solid foods such as apples and potatoes are over 50 percent water. As the water is drawn out of them the enzyme action (which spoils food) is suspended. Moisture and warmth are needed to start the enzymic action in full swing again.

In removing water from food, a combination of heat and warm moving air is best. We dry foods in the sun, in specially built dehydrators, or in the kitchen oven.

Heat from the sun. This is the most ancient method, and continues to be widely used. When I lived in the country we spread out corn and apples on clean sheets or feed sacks and dried them on the roof of the wood shed or the flat bed of the hay rack. To complete the drying we strung apples in loops that hung from the clothes line.

In Thailand I have seen bananas drying in shallow bowls with a glass over the top to focus the sun's rays. The same principle is used when old windows are placed over food to dry it in the sun's rays.

Specially built dehydrators. Dehydrators can be built of any size, any shape. Warm moving air dries the food on racks. A heating element provides the heat, allowing about 60 watts for each square foot of tray area. (150-watt light bulbs in porcelain sockets work fine.) A small 10-inch fan circulates the air through the food to the top where the hot moist air escapes through a vent that can be regulated. A hole in the box near the bottom (opposite the fan) provides a fresh air intake. Between 15 and 20 hours are required to dry a 40-pound load of halved prunes or peaches or a 20-pound load of sliced or shredded vegetables.

Oven drying. With the oven drying method it is difficult to control the temperature and moisture, but with experience it can be done. You should

— Prop the door open to control heat and let out moist air. (Gas oven 8 inches, electric oven ½ inch.)

— Check temperature with oven thermometer. (Do not use top unit in electric oven.)

— Aim at an even temperature of 125° to 150°. Too low a temperature will sour the food, while too high a temperature will harden it on the outside and thus prevent moisture inside from being released.

— Use trays made to fit the oven (wood frame with plastic screen, cotton netting, or wood slats tacked on). During World War II many people were using in the oven four trays that fitted in a rack. In this way about 10 pounds of fruit or vegetables could be dried at one time — more, if the vegetables were light-weight and leafy. (These same trays can be used to stand on the stove above the burners, or hang from the ceiling where the air is hot.)

— Not overload the trays, since this prevents good air circulation. For sliced fruit and vegetables (light weight) use one pound per square foot of tray space. For heavy halved fruit use about two pounds.

— Alternate the trays so that food will dry evenly. Remove food from around edges as it dries.

— Keep trays 3 inches from oven floor. Mineral oil on wood frames prevents food from sticking.

— Store in deep freeze any food which is not completely dried but which you have to remove.

Apricots, peaches and pears: Treat as indicated below to prevent discoloration. Remove pits, slice for drying in halves (pit side up). Dry at 150°. Fruit pliable and leathery when dry.

Prunes: Dry in halves or whole. If drying them whole, first "check" skins (see below).

Apples: Peel, core and cut in ¼-inch slices or rings. Treat for discoloration. Spread not more than ½ inch deep on trays. When dry they will be creamy white, pliable and springy. (Note that the late variety, firm, mature fruit is best for drying.)

Berries: When drying blackberries, dewberries, loganberries, or raspberries, spread ripe, firm fruit in thin layers on drying trays (cloth under the fruit will prevent sticking). Set oven at 120°, gradually increase this to 150°, then gradually lower temperature during last stage of drying. Cherries too can be dried at low temperatures.

Vegetables: Beans (shell or snap), beets, broccoli, cabbage, carrots, celery, corn, onions, peas, peppers, potatoes, pumpkin, spinach, squash, and tomatoes, have been successfully dried. (Cut up combinations of dried vegetables in small pieces for soup mixes, or make a nutritious vegetable powder for soups by grinding dried leafy and other vegetables to a fine powder.) Note that

— Vegetables should first be steamed in a wire basket above 2 inches of rapidly boiling water (cook until tender but firm). Test when cool. After drying they should be brittle, and should snap sharply when bent.

— Beans, peas, potatoes and spinach should be rinsed in cold water after being steamed.

— Most vegetables need to be steamed for 6 to 10 minutes. Exceptions are leafy greens and celery (3 to 4 minutes) and string beans and beets (15 to 30 minutes).

— Vegetables should be dried at temperatures ranging from a low of 115° to a high of 150°. Start shell beans, peas, potatoes, and peppers at low, gradually increase to high, and reduce to low for last hour of drying. Start leafy vegetables on high and gradually reduce to low.

— Pumpkin or squash should be cut into strips ½ inch wide and about ¼ inch thick. Peel, and remove seeds and pithy material. Steam until tender — about 6 to 8 minutes. Spread on trays ½ inch deep. Start drying at 150° to 160°, and cut temperatures to 120° during last hour. Change positions of drying trays often.

Meat and Fish: If you don't have a smokehouse to smoke meat, use your oven and dry it. To make *jerky*, remove fat and muscle from cheap cuts of beef shank, chuck, or venison. Cut in strips ½ inch thick and 1 inch wide, cutting along and not across the grain. Pound into the meat a seasoning of salt, pepper, oregano, marjoram, basil and thyme. Spread on wire racks in oven set at 120°, leaving door slightly open to permit moisture to escape. Turn over when half done. (It will take about 10 hours to dry.) Jerky is done when it is shriveled up and black, but it should be taken out of the oven when flexible enough to bend. It will get more brittle as it cools. (About 4 lb. of fresh meat will make 1 lb. of jerky.)

Cut fresh *salmon* in strips ¾ inch thick and cut squares 1½ inches x 2½ inches. Soak in brine (¼ cup salt to 1 qt. water) for one hour. Remove, sprinkle with salt and pepper, and brush with liquid smoke. Place on racks with air space between strips. Dry at 170° for 24 hours.

Hastening Drying, Preserving Color and Vitamins

With *fruits*, expose more of the surface of food to heat and air by pitting the apricots, quartering the pears, slicing the apples in rings, and peeling the peaches. Dip whole prunes, figs, and grapes in boiling water for 1 or 2 minutes to "check" skins, permitting moisture to escape.

Darkening of fruit occurs because certain chemicals within food unite with oxygen. To prevent this, you either

— Sulfur the fruit by soaking it for 15 minutes in a sulfur solution (3½ tablespoons sodium sulfite — from drug store — to one gallon water).

— Dip fruit in salt-water bath of 4 to 6 tablespoons salt to 1 gallon water for about 10 minutes.

— Precook fruit in steam or boiling water until it is tender but firm.

With *vegetables*, blanching or steaming them before drying helps preserve valuable vitamins, sets the color, hastens drying by loosening the cell structure and tissues. It also insures that the flavor will be better when the vegetables are cooked later. Keep vegetable pieces smaller than fruit. Shred, dice, or slice, keeping the pieces no thicker than a large pea (about ¼ inch).

Miscellaneous Drying Ideas

You can dry sheets of food in the oven. Try making prune, banana or apple sauce "leather" by making a puree and spreading it thin on a teflon cookie sheet. Peel off when dry and pliable, like leather. Cut with scissors in small strips for snacks. Try a combination of fruits (grated apples with banana puree over the top, for example) and dry until crisp. Apricot and pineapple blended together is good. So is sweetened banana puree spread thin over a layer of oatmeal on a cookie sheet and dried to a crisp cracker. Try berries of different kinds.

Cooked meat and vegetables can be mixed in a blender and the mixture dried out in sheets in the oven. This makes a delicious crisp cracker.

One outdoorsman uses a waffle iron (with plain sandwich grill on the bottom) to make dehydrated foods for hikes. He makes "main course" and "dessert" waffles in this way.

SALTING AND BRINING

Salting and brining is a simple, inexpensive method and requires no special equipment, materials or skill. In many rural areas, or when it isn't feasible to freeze, dry or can, this method is used to preserve both meat and vegetables. And if the electricity supply were cut off for a considerable period, this method would be a good way to prevent the spoilage of food in the deep freeze.

Vegetables

Fermentation of vegetables is the same as salting and brining. Details for fermenting string beans are shown below. Other vegetables suitable for this treatment are:

Cabbage	Turnips
Corn	Vegetable greens
Peas and lima beans	Onions
(unshelled)	Cucumbers
Carrots	Green and red
Cauliflower	peppers
Beets	

In the salting and brining of vegetables, bacteria feed on the sugars which are drawn from the vegetable material by the salt or brine, and in the process acid is produced.

General directions and precautions. Use any clean *containers* but metal ones — e.g., crocks, wooden barrels or kegs, glass fruit jars, or plastic buckets.

To keep the food pressed down in the containers use a *cover* of wood or a plate, or wooden cross pieces (from ice cream sticks) for glass jars. For a *weight* over the cover use a clean stone, paraffined brick, or a bottle filled with water.

As the curing proceeds, remove the *scum* which develops — otherwise it will use up acid produced from fermentation.

Fermenting vegetables. Fermented food sounds like something you wouldn't want to eat. But it's delicious! A German lady's fermented string beans I sampled had been bottled for over two years but they were a fresh green color, crisp and sour, like pickles.

Vegetables processed by fermentation are preserved without heating. This factor would preserve vitamins and minerals normally destroyed by the high temperatures necessary in other canning methods.

Equipment	*Ingredients*
Crock jar (five gallon)	Vegetables
Fruit jars (with glass lids)	Salt and water
Plate (or round hardwood board)	Fresh dill or the seeds
	Grape leaves
Weight (water in gallon jar)	Garlic and pickling spice
Cotton cloth (two squares)	

The process for making fermented food is similar to making sauerkraut. You put layers of vegetables, salt and spices in a crock and cover it with grape leaves to preserve the color. Next, add a cloth, a plate and a weight. In ten days to two weeks it will be ready to put into bottles. Here is the process in detail.

1. Pick the string beans when they are small, just as the bean is beginning to form. (Older beans will be soft inside and tough outside.) Cut in 2-inch pieces. Weigh the beans.

2. Measure the water needed to fill the crock (about 6 to 7 quarts). Divide equally into two containers.

3. One-half cup of salt (5 ounces) is needed for every 10 lb. of vegetables. Divide the required amount in equal parts and dissolve it in the two containers of water. (Water containing too little salt will make the beans soft instead of snappy crisp.)

4. In the bottom of the crock place one bunch of fresh dill with seeds attached. (If this is not available, use the seeds from packages.)

5. Fill the crock with several layers of the cut beans and pour salt water over them. When the crock is nearly filled with beans make a hole in the center and put in a handful of garlic (four or five whole garlics, each cut in two). Add one heaping tablespoon of pickling spice. Mix throughout the beans with a wooden spoon, or wash hands and arms and mix.

6. Put about four layers of overlapping grape leaves on top and cover the crock with a cotton cloth large enough to hang down over the edge of the crock for a few inches all around.

7. Over the cloth put an inverted plate, or a round hardwood board a little smaller than the crock. Weight it down with a gallon jar containing as much water as needed. Cover with a clean cloth to keep away gnats, etc.

8. When foam starts building up, skim it off carefully for about four or five days. A greyish or brownish scum comes up on the plate and cloth and if this is not removed it will destroy the fermentation acid and the beans will be soft. To remove scum, remove the weight and plate. Fold the cloth to the center, take it to the sink, wash it out, and replace cloth, plate and weight.

9. Shake the crock. If you hear no bubbling, the fermentation is complete. (It should take from 10 days to 2 weeks, depending on the temperature.) The beans are now ready to put in bottles. When taking them out of the crock or jars use a fork or a spoon and not the fingers, as you may start a new fermentation in that way. Use glass lids if available, or cellophane and metal ring. Fill jars to the very top with beans and with the juice from the crock, so that there is no room for air. Put them in a cool place on layers of paper so that any juice leaking out won't damage the shelf.

The beans are delicious with meat instead of pickles, or on sandwiches.

To make *sauerkraut*, it will take 25 or 30 lb. of cabbage for a 5-gallon crock. Use ½ cup of salt for every 10 lb. of grated cabbage. Put dill in the bottom of the crock, then layers of about 5 lb. of cabbage and one-fourth cup of salt. Repeat until crock is half full. Put in the garlic (as in the directions for fermenting beans) and finish filling the crock. Put on the inverted plate and weight and follow directions for keeping the scum off, as with beans. Fermenting has stopped when the small bubbles cease coming to the top. Then put the sauerkraut in bottles, using the juice in the crock to fill to within ½ inch of the top. (If there is not enough liquid from the kraut itself, finish filling the jars with a salt solution, using 2 tablespoons salt to 1 quart water.)

If the storage place is warm and damp it will be necessary to process the sauerkraut and the beans after the fermenting period. Process in a hot water bath with water at least an inch over the top of the jars. For quart jars, allow 30 minutes after the water begins to boil.

Fermentation of cabbage takes place best at about 60° to 65°. To achieve this it may be necessary to immerse the stone jar in a tub of cold water which you replace daily.

A good way to serve sauerkraut is to fry bacon, remove it from the grease and cut it in pieces. Pour sauerkraut into the bacon grease, add beaten eggs, and cook slowly. Serve the sauerkraut with pieces of bacon on top and a slice of bread.

Lamb and Mutton

Begin a couple of days after slaughter (after meat has been chilled to 32° to 34°). For the *brine cure* for 100 lb. of meat you will need:

8 lb. salt
2 lb. white or brown sugar
2 oz. saltpeter

Dissolve ingredients in 6 gallons of cold water. Pack the chilled, trimmed meat carefully and closely in a clean crock or other container and pour in cold brine (36° to 38°) until the pack begins to shift and float. Weight it down. Overhaul the meat in 3 to 5 days — that is, repack so that all pieces are exposed to brine. Thin cuts of meat take from 10 days to 2 weeks, legs and shoulders from 25 to 40 days.

The *dry cure* for 100 lb. of meat will require:

  5 lb. salt
  4 lb. sugar
  4 oz. saltpeter

Mix ingredients and sprinkle some of mixture on bottom of clean container. Reserve ⅓ of the mixture for when you overhaul the meat, i.e., repack to keep meat completely covered. Using the ⅔ rub and pat proportionate amounts on each piece of meat.

The meat may be left in the cure until you want to use it. Alternatively you may remove it for smoking, in which case observe the same schedule as that given above for the brine cure.

Note that for both brining and salting you must use salt which does not contain ingredients to prevent caking.

Smoking

Smoked meat has a very palatable flavor. Smoking is a simple process of "drying out" the meat. Smoking tends to inhibit bacterial action. Cool smoked meats need no refrigeration. If electricity should go off for a long period of time, meats in frozen storage could be thawed and smoked.

Most kinds of meat can be smoked — hams, fish, wild game (tougher cuts make good jerky — cut along the grain not across it), beef, lamb, turkey, chicken, and fresh homemade sausage stuffed in narrow muslin bags.

Types of smokers include: Small building, wooden barrel, box, old ice box, electric refrigerator, or a portable smoker from the sport shop that fits in the fireplace. Take care to make the smoker fire-resistant by lining the lower half with metal or asbestos. Holes to control ventilation and temperature are needed. Use a thermometer, and keep the temperature at about 90°. The meat can either be hung from hooks or spread out in small pieces on wire trays. Allow a 2-inch clearance around the sides of the smoker for circulation of air.

You can make smoke by electricity if you want to do it the easy way. Get electricity to your smoker and use a two-burner hot plate. Put some hardwood sawdust or chips in a gallon can over the burner (leave part of the bottom free of chips, since air is needed for combustion). If you don't have sawdust use a nonresinous limb (apple, cherry, maple or oak), but first remove the bark or the meat may have a bitter flavor. Don't have the limb touch the burner — put a frypan or piece of metal between the two.

If electricity is not available, dig a little pit and in it build a fire of hardwood chips. Have a flue (a tile or stovepipe) underground carrying the smoke to the barrel or box which contains the meat.

Smoking temperature and time vary for different kinds of meat. For kippered fish (with a high oil content) a "hot smoking" process is used with a temperature of 100° to 125° for 10 to 12 hours, which is then increased to 150° for 2 to 4 hours. "Cool smoking" of lamb takes 2 days at 100° to 120°. Other meats may take from one to two weeks.

To smoke cured meat, scrub it with hot water and a stiff brush and hang it up to drain and dry before putting it in the smoker.

CANNING

Before we had home freezers, canning was the most common way to preserve food. And it is still a good policy to have on hand bottles and lids with which to can fruits, vegetables and meat. Not only would we be ready to process food in the freezer in the event of a prolonged power failure, but we would be able to take care of food bargains as I once did years ago in California. Over the radio came the announcement that the machinery had broken down in a local cannery and that trainloads of vine-ripened tomatoes were being made available to the public at a very low price. We brought home enough for 200 quarts.

Processing the tomatoes in my six-quart canner would have taken considerable time. Instead we bottled them all in one afternoon, outside under the shade of a tree. We used two fifty-gallon metal barrels as "canners." We filled them with water, built a fire under each one, then:

1. Cleaned the jars and lids in hot water.
2. Scalded the tomatoes (one minute in hot water, then one minute in cold).

3. Skinned them and firmly packed them in quart bottles.

4. Added 1 teaspoon of salt per bottle, poured water in the bottle to within ½ inch of the top, and wiped off the seeds and pulp.

5. Put the flat lid on and screwed the band firmly tight.

6. Carefully lowered the jars into the barrel of water so that they didn't touch each other. (Laths separated the layers of bottles, and were also put under the first layer of bottles to keep them from touching the bottom.)

7. Kept hot water boiling around and over the top of all the bottles for about 35 minutes.

8. Removed the bottles and placed them on folded cloths. (The lids popped and went slightly concave, a spoon test on the center of the lid gave a clear ring, and we knew they were properly sealed.)

9. Carefully removed the bands and lined the jars up on the cool dark basement shelves.

We enjoyed these tomatoes for a long time, without having any spoilage.

One's bottling is not usually done in such large quantities, but the principles are the same whether the quantity is large or small.

Nutrition retention. When food is canned there is some loss of vitamins and enzymes that are destroyed by ordinary cooking temperatures. However, provitamin A is quite stable in canned fruit and vegetables and very stable in canned tomatoes.

The nutrition retention in food canned in a pressure cooker at a high temperature for a short time has been found to be about the same as when it is canned by processing in boiling water for a longer time. However, the pressure cooker method is surer for low acid foods — meats and vegetables.

Some vitamin loss must be expected in stored canned foods. For example:

— Vitamin C and thiamine in canned vegetables stored at 65° suffer a loss of up to 15 percent in a year. When stored at 80° the loss is about 25 percent in a year.

— Thiamine in canned meats may be reduced by as much as 30 percent in only six months when stored at 70°.

— Riboflavin is not affected by ordinary storage temperatures.

If we are going to "use what we store and store what we use" we must use canned foods in our daily menus in order to keep them properly rotated in our storage plan. Many people don't like to use canned foods to excess when fresh and frozen produce is available. A solution to this problem is to store an abundance of grains, seeds and nuts, legumes, etc., that dehydrate naturally, and then to sprout these foods for a vitamin supply in a time of emergency.

Canning without sugar. Honey syrup for canning is made from 1 part honey (mild, light kind) to 2 parts water. Bring to a rolling boil, skim and strain. Use as you would a sugar syrup.

Rhubarb will keep when cut in inch-long pieces, packed in jars and covered with water. Put a lid on the jar. No cooking or sealing is necessary.

This method for "pickling" grapes comes from the oldtimers in Southern Utah:

1. When the California grapes are at their best, pick the clusters.

2. With scissors, carefully cut off any bad ones or small green ones. (With this method, never pull grapes off the stem leaving a moist end.)

3. Do not wash the grapes.

4. Pack grapes in a keg or crock with stems up (so that they can be lifted out by stem).

5. Make a mixture of molasses and water (just enough molasses to tint the water caramel colored) and cover grapes with it.

6. Place keg in dark, cool place.

7. Keep grapes down in the liquid by placing wooden lid or plate on top to act as weight.

8. About Christmas time (after about four months) lift out a bunch of grapes, wash off and leave in cold water a short time. (The grapes sort of warm you up inside and are just a little nippy in taste.)

Canning wheat. When canning wheat, soak it for 12 to 15 hours. Drain, cover again with water, and boil for 15 minutes. Fill jars three-quarters full of wheat, add water to within ½ inch of top. Put on lid and screw band firmly tight. Process in pressure cooker for 35 minutes at 20 lb. pressure.

APPLIANCES AND EQUIPMENT

In preserving and preparing food, many people are fortunate enough to have an ideal combination — a modern kitchen and its appliances plus equipment used on the farm in grandma's time before "prepared" foods (that require only reheating) became a way of life.

If we had only the four survival foods to work with (or limited storage foods) it would be a great advantage in meal preparation to have ways to change the appearance, texture, and form of foods. A variety of equipment would help to make the meals more interesting for the partaker and more creative for the cook. In addition, having the means to preserve and store food eliminates waste and helps us take advantage of perishable food bargains at the market, or of home grown fruits and vegetables which generous neighbors and friends sometimes supply free in years of abundant crops.

In common with many other families, my family has budget problems. But our family expenditure and effort made in acquiring appliances, equipment and food constitute the wisest investments we have made. I give below a partial list of equipment for preserving and preparing food which we took with us in a move not long ago, after the family had grown up. (There were moments during the move when I questioned my sanity!)

To grind the grain:

   Electric stone grinding mill
   Hand grinding mill
   Big antique cereal grinder

Electric coffee grinder for cereal
Small hand coffee grinder
Seed and nut grinder

To cook the food:

Electric stove
Coal range (connected into the basement fireplace flue)
Two fireplaces with cast iron pot (to swing out on an
   arm over the fire)
Two-burner camp stove
Small gasoline stove
Charcoal barbecue and turning spit
Reflector oven
Gallon can containing heating unit consisting of a tightly-
   folded coiled newspaper pushed into a tuna can and
   soaked in paraffin wax (burns 1½ hours)
Heat tablets

Small electrical appliances:

Food blender
Electric mixer
Champion juicer
Electric carving knife
Toaster
Waffle iron

To keep foods cold:

Freezer
Three refrigerators
Two ice chests
Thermos jugs, from gallon to pint
Ice cream freezer

For home canning, freezing, drying, etc.:

Home dehydrator
Fruit canners
Jars and lids
Vegetable steamer
Freezer bags
Hand juicer

Colander
Sauerkraut slicer
Crocks

Miscellaneous:

Meat grinder
Food and oven thermometers
Seed sprouting trays
Small and large bread pans
Roasting pan, dripper, dish pans
Small and large muffin tins
Barbecue forks
Corn popper
Hand bread toaster
Paper and/or plastic cups, plates and spoons
Stainless steel camp dishes
Graters (all sizes) and strainers
Ice cream scoop
Wire bee hat and smoker
Gallon water jugs
(We had sold the big apple cider press and milk separator)

To grow a garden:

Pick, shovel, rake and a hoe
Wheelbarrow, garden hose
Garden tiller
Seed flats and bands

CHAPTER 10

Food Storage

WINTER STORAGE OF GARDEN VEGETABLES

Farmers and others have long used their ingenuity in finding ways to store vegetables from one harvest season to the other. Some of the methods they have devised would help us all in this matter of setting up a more adequate food storage program.

When I grew up in the country, pits and cellars were interesting places to me, with their sloping (and sliding) doors, their various kinds of entrances. Some pits were entirely underground, some halfway, while some storage places were above ground. Some were under the house, some by the house, some out in the field. Above-ground "pits" were cone-shaped, or igloo-shaped mounds, either big or little, covered with straw and soil. Celery and cabbage were stored in trenches.

While frozen foods and supermarkets reduce the need for this type of storage, some modern families enjoy the convenience and economy of buying vegetables in quantity and properly storing them on a small scale in their garages or basements or outside.

Basement Storage

If you have central heating you can partition off a room on the north or east side of the house and insulate it for storage. You need one or two windows for cooling and ventilating. Equip the room with shelves. Removable slatted flooring facilitates air circulation. Sprinkle water or wet sawdust on the floor to raise the humidity.

For preference store your vegetables in wood crates rather than in bins. In your storage room, vegetables could be kept in a large metal milk can, with the lid partly off. They will stay as crisp as they would in the crisper in the refrigerator. Root crops also keep crisp in moist sand and in peat or sphagnum moss.

Probably better than any of the above is to keep vegetables
(root crops) in polyethylene bags or box liners and store in a
cool place. For ventilation, cut about four ¼-inch holes in the
sides of each bag or liner. Tie the bags, and fold over the tops
of box liners.

Outside Storage

In many parts of the country, vegetables can be left in the
garden where they grew. One family near Portland, Oregon,
where the average winter temperature is about 40°, reports that
for the past ten years they have left their vegetables in the
ground. In only two of the years were the frosts severe enough
to ruin the vegetables. They planted late crops of cabbage and
cauliflower that matured at different times during the winter.

If winters are severe, and you want to dig your vegetables
and store them in pits, etc., be sure to

— Stagger your planting so some crops mature late in the
fall.

— Leave them in the ground as long as possible.

— Dig the vegetables when the soil is dry.

— Cut plant tops ½ inch above the crown.

— Wash vegetables, but dry them off before storing.

— Protect them from drying winds.

— See that vegetables are cool before putting them in storage.

For *storage places,* you can use

—A wooden barrel placed on its side and covered with straw
and soil.

— An old refrigerator buried in the ground with its door
facing upwards.

— Small cone-shaped outdoor mounds for storing potatoes,
carrots, beets, turnips, salsify, parsnips, cabbage, or winter
apples or pears. Directions:

1. Choose a well-drained location.

2. Make a nest of straw, leaves, or other bedding material on the ground.

3. Bury the vegetables (small quantities of different kinds), covering with more bedding.

4. Cover the mound with about 4 inches of soil and firm the soil with the back of the shovel.

5. Dig a shallow drainage ditch around the mound.

6. Allow for ventilation into the mound by having a small amount of the bedding material extend up through the soil to the top of the pile. Cover the opening with a board or with sheet metal to protect it from rain.

Note that pits or mounds should be in a different place every year, since leftovers in used pits usually are contaminated.

Large outdoor pits are not practical unless the winter temperatures in your area average 30° or below. If you use them remember that

— Dirt floors help maintain proper humidity.

— Underground cellars maintain a more uniform temperature. (They also can serve as storm or fallout shelters.)

— Members of a family or group in the same vicinity could share a large storage pit.

Miscellaneous Information

The dampness of outdoor pits encourages decay and is not recommended for sweet potatoes, pumpkins and squash, onions, or peppers.

Sweet potatoes, pumpkins and squash should be stored in a dry place at 55° to 60°. For better keeping, harden the rinds and heal surface cuts by curing (by a heater or furnace) for 10 days at 80° to 85°. (Acorn squash is the exception — curing makes it stringy and orange-colored, whereas it should be dark green.)

Onions sprout and decay at high temperatures in high humidity. Store in open, loosely-woven bags at room temperature or slightly cooler.

Peppers (green) will keep for 2 or 3 weeks in a box with a polyethylene liner at 45° to 50°. (Make twelve to fifteen ¼-inch holes in the liner.)

Potatoes. Late crop potatoes will keep for several months in a cool, dark place at 45° to 50° with good ventilation. Higher temperatures cause sprouting and shriveling. Lower temperatures may give potatoes a sweet taste. Light causes greening and lowers eating quality.

Apples. Apples keep best at about 32° where temperature remains the same and the air is rather moist. Do not store apples and vegetables together in the same place.

Parsnips. Leave parsnips in the ground. The flavor and texture improve with frost.

Cabbage. Pull cabbage up by the roots and place head down in a long mound, above ground level. Cover with straw and soil and dig a drainage ditch around the mound.

Storing the Four Foods

Packaging the four survival foods — wheat, milk powder, honey and salt — in five-gallon cans has been a project of different groups who have been awakened to the need for emergency storage. Each can contains one month's food supply for one adult person: 27 lb. of wheat, 5 lb. of powdered skim milk, 3 lb. of honey, up to 1 lb. of salt.

Advantages of such a storage plan are that

— Premeasurement of the foods on a monthly one-person basis, plus compactness of storage, makes it easy to store exactly what is needed for a given number of people.

— It helps to insure balance in the emergency diet, since all four items tend to be used up in the correct proportions. When the items are stored in separate containers, they often are used up in wrong proportions and inadequately replaced.

Insect Control

Use of chemicals. Pre-storage treatment of wheat is normally not necessary so long as it is low-moisture (less than 10 percent moisture), hard, winter wheat which has been properly cleaned, is placed in a proper container, and is stored under the right conditions. The most moisture-proof can for grain storage is the common five-gallon square can with a paint-can type clamp lid. The cover-over clamp type lid should be used only in dry climates.

However, some people prefer to treat the grain before storage. Opinions differ as to the best method. Some advocate displacing the air with carbon dioxide formed from dry ice. Others says that wheat thus treated has been found later to be contaminated with weevil because of the moisture introduced with the dry ice. (Certainly, any crust or formation of natural ice should be brushed off dry ice before it is put in the can.) Some advocate fumigating grain with carbon tetrachloride. (See Max L. Sweat's article "Home Storage Simplified," *The Instructor*, May 1969, pages 187-188 and inside back cover.) Others see this usage as involving too many dangers, especially in its application by amateurs. As in many other areas, the answer may lie in how skillfully the product is used.

If one is concerned about the possible need to treat his wheat, perhaps he would be best advised to consult the local office of the Food and Drug Administration or the County Agricultural Extension Office. Officials there should be able to give advice based not only on up-to-date scientific information but also on local conditions (humidity, etc.).

Use of heat. If wheat has been infested with insects they can be eradicated by the following method. Place not more than ¾ inches wheat in a shallow pan and put the pan in a 150° oven for 20 minutes. Leave the oven door open slightly to prevent over-heating. This treatment will destroy all stages of insect pests if the wheat is thoroughly heated.

Moisture, Light and Heat

Moisture. To prevent reproduction of insects, store wheat where the air has a moisture content of 10 percent or below, in which conditions it will keep indefinitely in a sealed can. Note that if moisture is allowed to come in contact with dry milk the flavor and odor of the milk will change.

Moisture rusts cans. To prevent this, paint the outside of the can with oil-based house paint.

If your wheat has too high a moisture content you can treat it with heat in a shallow pan with the same process as that shown above for insect control.

Light. Some vitamins are damaged by light, which is the reason for dark milk bottles, pill bottles, etc. Keep all bottled foods in a dark place.

Heat. Canned foods will keep twice as long at 40° as at 70°. Where possible, keep storage area temperatures from going above 70° and below freezing point (32°).

Food Spoilage

Foods spoil because of enzymic action and decomposition by mold, yeast, and bacteria. Bacteria and bacterial spores (which are more resistant than bacteria but germinate into bacteria under appropriate conditions) are present on all foods, and in water, air and soil.

Food poisoning arises from

— Chemicals (additives, pesticides, etc.).

— Food itself (mushrooms, sea fish, etc.),

— Bacteria (primarily botulinus and staphylococcus bacteria multiplying in meat, fish, eggs, milk and milk products, and in canned low-acid vegetables).

We keep food from spoiling by

— Eliminating air (e.g., replacing air with water vapor — by boiling — or with gas, see above). (However, it is noted that some bacteria (botulinus) grow only in the absence of air. High heat must be used to destroy this class of bacteria.)

— Reducing the moisture content (drying, smoking).

— Killing the bacteria (complete sterilization in canning process).

— Stopping or slowing down action of enzymes and bacterial growth (freezing).

— Salting.

Off-flavors of food are not always indicative of spoilage but should be looked upon with suspicion.

Spoilage other than that referred to above is generally associated with

— Rancidity of fats.

— Slime and mold formation.

— Fermentation.

— Damaged containers.

Particularly dangerous bacterial spoilage is indicated by

— Off-odors in food.

— Sour or bitter taste in bland foods.

— Gassy, spurting liquid and bulging cans of food.

— Color changes in canned meat. This refers mostly to the bulk of the meat. (Blackening of the edges in contact with the metal of the can, such as often noted in canned corned beef, is due to chemical reaction between the iron of the can and the sulfur of the food. It is not generally harmful. As this process introduces iron into the food it may actually contribute to iron in the diet. The chief consideration is whether gas or off-odors are present and the major portion of the meat is discolored.)

Boiling is one way which may be helpful in determining whether canned meat is safe. Heat brings out the characteristic odor of spoiled meat. Without tasting it, immediately destroy any canned meat that has an unusual odor. Be sure to dispose of it where it cannot be eaten by humans or animals.

To test a *smoked ham*, run a sharpened end of a stiff wire along the bone to the center of the ham. If the wire brings out a sweet odor the meat is sound. If it brings out an unpleasant odor, cut the ham open and examine for spoilage.

Temperatures are very important in the matter of food spoilage. Foods kept at in-between temperatures for a long time (e.g., carried to a picnic or left on steam tables at restaurants) are ideal conditions for the reproduction of the organisms that cause food poisoning. One way to avoid this is to carry food in an insulated box. Particularly avoid cream — or pudding — filled pastries which are more than a day old and have not been refrigerated. Remember that bacteria are on their merry way of decomposing foods whenever the foods are warm and moist.

ROTATION OF FOODS

In their unorganized eagerness to store against emergency, many people have wasted untold amounts of food because of failure to follow a rotation plan. One must remember that while grains and dried foods generally come under the *permanent* food storage plan, canned or bottled foods come under a *rotating* plan. We need both types of items in storage.

On a rotating plan, pretend you are operating a food market. Markets don't stock food that doesn't sell. Similarly, you should *store what you use and use what you store.* As food items are used, replace them with fresh supplies. Put the fresh always at the back of the stockpile, and keep older supplies in front.

A convenient way to rotate canned foods is to store them on specially constructed shelves which slope toward the front and on which the cans lie on their sides. As a can is removed from the front the line slides forward. New stock is placed at the back.

STORAGE OF CANNED FOODS

Canned foods stored for a long time are safe to eat provided the cans are not bulged or leaking. However, over a period of time chemical reaction in the cans alters the flavor, texture and nutritive value. Following is a list showing the safe periods for the principal canned fruits and vegetables (unfrozen). Since temperatures vary greatly for stored foods, the shelf life in any instance is necessarily an estimate.

Six Months	*One to Two Years*
Grapefruit juice	Cherries
Orange juice	Berries
Fruit juices in general	Prunes
	Plums
	Tomato juice
	Roast beef

Two to Three Years	Spinach
Peaches	Greens
Pears	Tomatoes
Apricots	
Applesauce	*Four to Five Years*
Beets	Peas
	Corn
Three to Four Years	Lima beans
Carrots	Tuna fish
Green beans	Corned beef

Canned milk will keep two or three years if agitated every 30 days.

FOOD STORAGE QUESTIONS AND ANSWERS

In an excellent article and accompanying chart published in the *Instructor* magazine for May, 1969, Max L. Sweat gives some suggestions for a food storage program. Here are some further ideas and tips based on questions asked from time to time.

My only storage space is a hot attic. Try rearranging your storage items. Store extra bedding, paper goods and clothing in the attic, and make room for food where it is cooler. The northeast part of your house should be the coolest.

We live in a two-room apartment.[1] In the winter when the rooms are heated, stack the food against an outside wall. In the summer move it to an inside wall or closet, the coolest place in the room. One family put their box springs and mattress over permanent wheat storage which was housed in five-gallon cans.

Our only storage space is a damp basement. Always put slats of wood between the cement and the items stored, as the cement has a tendency to "sweat." If the basement is damp, paint the outside of the food storage can with oil-based house paint.

We move so often, it's hard to store food. Store wheat in five-gallon cans for ease of transportation. Sell your furniture if you must — you'll replace that, but maybe not your stored food if you should once dispose of it.

What do I do if food has weevil in it? As with whole grains, beans, cereals, nut meats and similar foods may be heated in

[1]Esther Clark Naylor, "Storing Food in a Two-Room Apartment. (*Relief Society Magazine,* August, 1948).

the oven at a temperature of 150° for 20 minutes. (For details see Insect Control, above.) Infested raisins, dried prunes and home-dried fruits may be placed in a small cheesecloth bag and dipped into boiling water for six seconds. Thoroughly dry the contents of the bag before storing them in pest-proof containers.

How can I clean some uncleaned wheat? Use a hand sieve made of screen similar to wire door screen.

Some say dry skim milk should only be stored for six months. Is this true? From reliable sources I have the following reports: "I have had dry skim milk in quart jars on my basement shelves for seven years and it is still good." "Whole dry milk was delicious after 8 years." "Vacuum packed skim milk tasted fresh after 14 years." Some say dry milk has a "flavor drop" after long storage, but it is still usable. In any case keep it in airtight containers in a cool place.

How long will honey keep? Perhaps indefinitely under proper storage conditions. Reports indicate that the quality of honey kept in cans for five to ten years is not affected even though the honey solidifies. (To melt the honey, put the can in a large pan of hot water.)

Some honey dealers dilute their honey with water. This product will not store long and will tend to ferment. Before you invest in large quantities be sure you are getting good honey.

What is the best way to keep a record of food I have stored? Here is a simple form:

OUR FAMILY FOOD RESERVE

Kind of food	Amount stored	Date purchased	Suggested replacement date

Checklists and records will help keep a balance in the supplies on hand. Don't estimate or guess. You may think you have a year's supply whereas in reality you may have sufficient for only a few months.

Bob R. Zabriskie's book *Family Storage Plan* (Bookcraft, Inc., Salt Lake City, Utah) contains ten forms for keeping records of storage foods. With these forms you can see visually what you have stored, what has been used, and what needs replacing. (The book also gives suggestions for storing vegetables, fruit, cheese, eggs, butter, etc.)

STARTING A FOOD STORAGE PROGRAM

When we embark on an emergency food storage program there is rarely enough money to do all we want and need to, even if one digs into the children's savings acounts — as one might well be justified in doing for such a compelling reason. When my family reached this point we found we could raise just $400. We wanted to store other necessities as well as the survival four. Deciding what to buy was a real budgeting problem. It might help others to know how we spent this money.

In shopping around by phone we discovered that at the feed store we could get hard Montana wheat for $4 a 100-lb. sack, but it was ungraded and uncleaned. (Recleaned was about $8.) I knew that we needed wheat with a moisture content of under 10 percent and with protein content of over 12 percent, and I learned that the state Grain Inspection Office would run a test for about $2.75. I took a 2½-quart sample there and it qualified, so we bought five sacks. (This saved money. We cleaned the wheat ourselves.) Through one of the markets we bought some recleaned high-protein wheat.

From the dairy we bought non-fat dry milk for about 26 cents a pound in 50-lb. plastic-lined paper bags which would keep out moisture for some time but would soon need to be replaced by moisture-proof cans, as we live in a rainy area. (The "instant-crystal" milk in vacuum-packed tins was more expensive.) The market had good clover honey in 5-lb cans for $1.04.

Containers for storing foods were hard to find. A can company I contacted would not sell in orders of less than $200, and even then each 5-gallon can would have cost about 78 cents. In the end I obtained some one-gallon jars and 30-lb. tins free from the school cafeteria, the bakery, and the restaurant.

We knew of course that we were not putting away a year's supply with this money. We still had made no provision for extra shoes and boots and other clothes for the whole family. With five growing children there seemed no end to the need on that score. When the food was all bought I realized that I had even forgotten to allow money for raisins — the children loved them, and it wouldn't have seemed normal not to scrape up black spots when I mopped the kitchen floor.

With all the reservations, then, and recognizing that perhaps no two families would have spent the money in exactly the same way, here is a statement of how I spent $400 for survival preparedness.

Amt. Spent		Quantity — Remarks
$100	*Wheat*	Ten 100-lb. sacks of recleaned tested wheat, and five 100-lb. sacks of uncleaned (to be cleaned by hand).
$100	*Dry Milk*	400 lb. for all my milk drinkers.
$ 50	*Honey*	About 250 lb. I like white honey, but dark, unstrained honey contains more vitamins and minerals.
$ 5	*Salt*	
$255		—Only $145 left. What else will I buy?
$ 20	*Peanut butter*	20 lb.
	Tomato juice	3 cases
$ 25	*Soy beans* *Brown rice* *Green dried peas*	
	Millet	Peas were only $5 a hundred lb. at the feed store.
$ 60	*Soap, etc.*	90 cakes of hand soap², 90 lb. laundry soap, 4 gallons chlorox, 6 packages sal soda.

---

²This goes rancid after several years. Long-term rotation is desirable.

$360		—$40 left. How will I make it stretch?
$ 10	*Molasses* *Cooking oil* *Vitamin pills* *Dry yeast*	
$ 10	*Toilet tissue*	Only about a third of what I need for a year.
$ 10	*Flavorings*	Bouillon cubes; vanilla, mint and almond flavoring; food coloring; brown sauce; soy sauce.
	Seeds	The usual ones for planting, plus watercress, parsley, escarole and mustard greens; also alfalfa seeds to sprout, and seseame seeds for use in breads and candies, etc.
$ 10	*Miscellaneous*	Candles, white muslin yardage, apple cider vinegar, tooth paste and brushes, corn starch for chafed skin, vaseline, mentholatum, and used bottles and cans for dried foods and water storage.
$400		(Well spent—for my peace of mind!)

CHAPTER 11

Water for Survival

We have said a good deal about the storage and preparation of food for survival conditions. What about water? Water makes up over half the volume of our blood, which carries food elements to every living cell. In an emergency our need for water may well be greater than that for food.

No Food, No Panic

People who have never gone without food, except perhaps for short periods during mild illnesses, frequently view the possibility of doing so with horror, almost with panic. But there is no justification for this reaction, for it is possible to go without food for many days without any ill effects as long as one has water. For example, I went without food for 48 hours and felt fine, and a friend of mine was happy and energetic after not eating for six days. I have read of people who claim to have been without food for periods ranging from 23 to 102 days and are still living and healthy.

Thus, while circumstances may prevent us from having three meals a day, it is reassuring to know that a person in normal health could still go about his work in that situation.

Far from dreading abstinence from food, some seek it. Some claim physical benefits from going without food; others abstain for spiritual reasons. Whatever the reason for going without food, as long as we have water we can relax and know that we will survive for a considerable length of time. Hence if we have stored the minimum amount of water needed for our family, if we know of other local sources, and if we are aware of small ways to conserve water, we can feel relatively easy about this area of survival.

Normal Water Consumption

The amount of water we use in our homes has increased tremendously over the years. As an example of a modern American city I discovered that for Portland, Oregon, where I live, the average consumption amounted to 147 gallons a day per inhabitant in 1967. As recently as twelve years before that (1955-56) it was 114 gallons.[1]

While recovering from the shock of these statistics I meditated on the availability of water around the world, past and future. In my childhood we didn't waste water. It had to be carried up in buckets from the ditch in front of the house. Sudsy wash water was saved to scrub the porches and floors, or to douse over cabbage plants to rid them of bugs. Greasy dishwater went to the hogs. Saturday-night bath water from the tin tub (in which more than one person had bathed) was carried out and dumped on the lawn or trees. Water which had been used to rinse out the milk buckets was poured on the geraniums in the window, and mineral-rich whey from cottage cheese provided fertilizer for plants in the door yard. A measured amount of water went into the dish pan or washbasin. There was no waste of running water to get the desired temperature, hot or cold.

Meantime the demand of plant life for water was minimized by frequent cultivation of garden rows to bring the water up, while a mulch of grass clippings and leaves around trees reduced evaporation of water.

Thus was water conservation practiced indoors and out, at least in rural communities. Today, unless we are concerned about paying the water bill, we rarely economize on its use.

Abundant pure water is a blessing. This fact came into sharp focus for me as I passed the city water taps in Agra, India, early one morning and saw the migration of people with bright pans and buckets to get their daily water supply. The sign above the washbasin in one of the newer hotels in New Delhi also spoke volumes. It read: "Don't drink or wash your teeth in this water."

---

[1]Portland Water Bureau, Portland, Oregon.

In Manila, I saw horse-drawn carts taking barrels of water to distressed areas during a serious drought. In Cairo, Egypt, the bus driver stepped off to get a cool drink of water from a jug on the sidewalk, using a tin cup placed there for public use. Jugs to catch precious rain water for drinking, surrounded homes I saw in Thailand and Egypt.

Possible Water Shortage

A temporary extreme water shortage in the United States could silence our automatic washers, dishwashers, garbage disposers, toilets, showers, and sprinkling systems. But we could still live on if we had drinking water and a minimum amount stored for household use.

What could cause a water shortage? It might be a drought, as prophesied in the scriptures. Earthquakes or bombings could break water lines and disrupt service. Nuclear fallout or contamination from bacteria could render normal supplies unusable.

Dehydration, ill health, and ultimately death result if the body's minimum water requirements are not met. Under good conditions man can survive for only about ten days without water.

Water in an Emergency

The body of a male adult contains more than 10 gallons of water. The loss of 10 percent body weight in water is disabling; the loss of 15 to 20 percent body weight in water could be fatal. The body normally uses about 2½ quarts of water daily.

Water storage. At such a rate of consumption it would be difficult to store sufficient water to last for, say, a year. In the expectation and hope that normal supplies would not be cut off for more than about a two-week period at a time we should store as an absolute minimum one quart a day for each adult to cover such a period. Twenty gallons for each family member would be a safer figure, on the basis that, while this would not last very long, should the emergency be prolonged one would hope to obtain water from other sources before the storage supply was exhausted.

When storing water, add a bleach solution containing 5¼ percent of sodium hypochlorite. Such solutions are available

in grocery stores. The following table shows the proper amount
to add to water.

Amount of Water	Amount of Solution to Add to	
	Clear Water	*Cloudy Water*
1 quart	2 drops	4 drops
1 gallon	8 drops	16 drops
5 gallons	½ teaspoon	1 teaspoon

Add the chlorine solution to the water and stir, then let
the mixture stand for thirty minutes. After this length of time
the water should still have a distinct but not excessive taste
or smell of chlorine. If this taste or smell is not present, add
another dose of the solution to the water and let the water stand
another fifteen minutes.[2]

Containers for water storage. Bottles of heavy odorless
plastic with tight-fitting caps are preferred for storing water.
Glass jugs or bottles with screw tops can be used. Metal containers tend to give water an unpleasant taste.

Emergency sources of water supply. Bottled water, stored
canned fruit juices, water in home hot-water tanks and toilet
tanks, would help meet the need for liquids.

Activities when water is scarce. You can help to reduce
the need for water as well as seek to increase the supply. When
water is scarce, keep quiet to reduce perspiration. Note that
anything that acts as a laxative may deplete the system of moisture. Smoking heightens the need for fluid. Carry a clean button
or pebble in your mouth to decrease the sensation of thirst. If
you are outdoors, unprotected from the sun, dig a trench two
or three feet deep (preferably when it is cool), running east and
west, and lie down in the shade during the heat of the day.
After being thirsty for a long time, when you find water avoid
nausea by drinking only small amounts at a time. Since the skin
will absorb water, clothes can be wrung out in undrinkable water
and placed on the skin.

---

[2]*U.S. Department of Agriculture Bulletin No. 77* (Home and Garden),
p. 315.

Collecting rain water. In an emergency you may need to know how to collect rain water. Scout troops have used the following method. Spread out clothing over sticks or limbs about six inches above ground. Shape a sag in the middle of the cloth and put any kind of clean container under the lowest part of the sag. Most of the water will funnel to this sag and collect in the container. Palm leaves or similar large leaves added along the edges of the clothing will increase the area of the collecting surface.

Finding water. Even more "know-how" is required to find water in the ground. One way is to use a solar still. In the desert you can get up to three pints of water a day from a bowl-shaped hole in the ground and a piece of clear plastic over the top with a weight in the center and a container underneath. (See diagram.) Heat from the sun will cause moisture to condense on the bottom of the plastic and this will drip into the container. Moisture condenses even faster if you drop water-holding desert plants under the plastic. Even impure water, or salty water in the bottom of a boat, can be made pure by this method of vaporizing and condensing.[3]

SOLAR STILL. Dig a pit 4 feet wide by 3 feet deep. Put a shallow container in the center. If possible, rig a tube from this up to the edge of pit. Stretch clear plastic over pit, with a rock in the center to form a cone directly over container. (Split cactus stems laid around inside will improve yield.) Any kind of water poured around pit will help. Solar heat evaporates water that will condense on plastic and drip into pan. Draw water through tube to avoid disturbing still. Make several stills if these are your sole source.

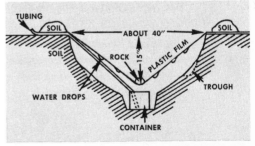

[3]Taken from Boy Scouts of America *Fieldbook for Men and Boys* (p. 315), whose diagram and photograph are here reproduced with permission.

Willows, cottonwoods and green vegetation mark permanent water sources. Cacti store fluid which can be used for an emergency drink. Follow game trails, watch birds head for water. Look for man-made wells or a dry bed stream. Dig down two feet — and if you find damp sand, dig deeper. Mop up dew before sunup from metal surfaces. Or twist chunks of fresh fish in a cloth, squeeze out the juice, and drink it.

How to purify water. Is the water safe to drink? If this is in question, boil the water for five minutes or more. For a fresh taste, pour the boiled water back and forth between two utensils, or add a pinch of salt.

Here are some miscellaneous suggestions on purifying and sweetening water.

Water purifying tablets: Follow directions on package.

If you have ordinary household 2 percent tincture of iodine in your home medicine chest you can use it to purify small quantities of water. Add three drops of tincture of iodine to each quart of clear water, or six drops to each quart of cloudy water, and stir thoroughly. For a gallon, add 12 drops for clear water, 24 drops for cloudy water.

To sweeten water, drop several bits of charred hardwood from the campfire into a boiling pot of water, simmer it for twenty minutes, then strain it or let it settle.

CHAPTER 12

Other Necessities for Emergency Use

Other things besides food and drink may be needed in an emergency situation. To be independent and self-sustaining we should store items for comfort, health, cleanliness, and well-being. Even if we ourselves should not find the need for some of these stored items, it would be a satisfying experience to be able to respond to a call from others for help. In fact, helping others always imparts a satisfaction — even a zest for living. This would probably be even more noticeable in a time of emergency, when we would need all the incentives to positive living.

Here then are items I suggest for emergency storage, apart from food.

Keeping Clean

— 20 lb. of laundry soap and 15 cakes of hand soap per person; tincture of green soap for washing injured parts (sal soda will extend the soap supply).

— Bath towels, wash cloths, dish towels and plenty of soft, clean rags.

— Ammonia, lye and borax — for soap making (see instructions below for making soap).

— Tooth paste, tooth brushes.

— Shaving supplies.

— Shoe polish.

— A broom or two.

— Window cleaner.

First Aid

— First-aid dressings, sterile gauze, adhesive tape, one-inch compresses, etc.

— Clinical thermometer.

— Rubbing alcohol (70 percent) — one pint, for bruises, sprains, etc.

— Hot water bottle, ice bag.

— Oil of cloves — for toothache.

— Baking soda, for eyewash — dissolve one scant teaspoonful in a glass of hot water; allow it to cool before use.

— Petrolatum (not medicated).

— Sterile castor oil or mineral oil.

— Additional items: Tourniquet, three feet of soft rubber tubing, blunt scissors, tongue blades, suturing kit.

Home Nursing

— Apple cider vinegar.

— Boric acid.

— Baby bottles, nipples.

— Bed pan, ear syringe, eye dropper.

— Empty capsules for medicine, etc.

— Kaopectate and kaolin clay — for diarrhea (clay for enema also).

— Mustard — for a plaster.

— Tincture of benzoin — for use in the vaporizer.

Comfort and Health

— Calamine, sunburn lotion.

— Foot remedies — corn and bunion plasters.

— Corn starch for alleviating chafing.

— Epsom salts and acid-stomach remedy.

— Hand lotion, make-up.

— Pills — vitamins, minerals, cod liver oil, aspirins.

— Sanitary napkins.

— Talcum powder, baby oil.

— Cleansing tissues and cold remedies.

Waste Disposal

— Two large 50-gallon drums — for human waste, one for liquid, one for solid (cover with lime).

— Lime.

— Spray for flies.

— Toilet tissue — 50 rolls a year per person.

Clothing

— Walking shoes and boots.

— Men's work clothes, socks.

— Women's sweaters, underwear, house dresses.

— Patterns for moccasins, house shoes, gloves and mittens.

— Silk kerchiefs (these have many uses — head scarfs for young and old, slings, etc.).

Bedding

— Sheets, pillow slips, pillows.

— Blankets, mattress pad.

— Baby blankets, rubber sheet.

Yardage and Sewing Supplies

— Bolt of white muslin material for sheeting.

— Flannel, gingham, denim, etc.

— Scissors, sewing needles, machine needles.

— Straight pins, safety pins.

— Thread (all colors), hooks and eyes, snaps, elastic, zippers.

Fuel

— Coal, wood briquets — or oil for the furnace.

— Try making charcoal from fruit pits or willows.

— Black walnuts make a good fuel. Old tires make a hot fire.

— Make newspaper "logs" using six sections (five double
sheets in each section) for each log. With double sheets
folded to page size, fold in halves once, then again, each
section separately. Stack the sections up, alternating cut
sides with folded ones, and with the bottom section extending out about 4 inches. Roll very tight, and secure
in the center of the roll with a piece of florist's wire. Four
logs last about an hour.

Lights

— 365 large candles — 4½ to 5 hours' burning time each.

— Kerosene or white gasoline lantern and fuel.

— Flashlights and batteries.

Seeds

— Alfalfa, beets, cabbage, carrots, chives, cucumbers, garlic,
green peas, leaf lettuce, mustard greens, onion, parsley,
radishes, spinach, squash, string beans, tomato, turnip
greens, watercress.

Note: When buying seeds, specify *untreated* so that they
can be either eaten (sprouted) or planted. Store them
in sealed containers. Seeds will keep for five years in
hermetically sealed cans.

Grinding the Grain

— A small stainless steel, stone mill.

— Electric coffee grinders can sometimes be converted into
wheat mills.

— The blender will grind small amounts of grain.

Equipment for Food Preparation

— Fireplace with iron stand for cooking.

— Open-fire kitchen range (could be moved outside in summer, and fruit canned under the fruit trees).

— Charcoal burner, reflector ovens, two-burner campstove.

— Home dryers, smoke house, or small dryers that fit in the fireplace — the type made for smoking jerky.

— Old fashioned meat grinders, crocks, canners, pitters and peelers may be used again. Don't throw them away.

Miscellaneous

— Rat poison.

— Rope (has many uses).

— Guns (for protection).

SOAP-MAKING

Equipment

For making soap you will need

— Container to make the soap in — 6-quart size or larger. It is best to use enamel, earthenware or granite containers, as the lye used in soap-making eats metal.

— Wooden stick or spoon to stir the soap.

— Fine sieve or cheesecloth to strain the fat.

— Molds to pour the soap in, either enamel or glass, lined with waxed paper or a damp cloth. A box, milk cartons, or small glass molds of any kind can be used. (If you don't want to use a mold, leave the soap in the pan until it sets, then turn it out and cut it in chunks.)

Directions for Making Soap

For ingredients, you will need:

> 10 cups animal fat — melted, strained and clarified
> 1 pound can lye[1]
> 5 cups rain water or soft water
> ½ cup powdered borax
> ½ cup ammonia

---

[1]In the early days lye water for soap was made by pouring boiling water over wood ashes, then straining it.

Use only animal fat. It can be rendered from meat fat. Don't overheat it. Strain in a fine sieve or a cheesecloth. To wash the salt out of fat which is salty, put the fat in a pan, cover it with cold water, and heat it. Allow it to cool, skim off the fat, and the salt and sediments will go to the bottom.

Now only five easy steps remain:

1. Warm fat to consistency of warm honey, so that it can be poured into lye mixture. (If fat is too hot it will curdle the soap.)

2. Put the 5 cups of water in the container.

3. Add the lye to the cool water and stir vigorously until it is dissolved. (Don't stand over the mixture.) Add the ammonia and borax, one at a time. Continue stirring until the mixture is cool. (Lye heats the water.)

4. Pour the fat into the lye mixture very slowly. Stir continuously for 15 minutes or until it is thick and creamy. (Don't over-stir.)

5. Pour the mixture into molds or flat pans, then allow it to stand for a day or so until it is set. Cut it into bars while it is medium soft, then wrap it in wax paper. It is ready to use in about a week. Some advise it should not be used for several months.

Variations. For laundry soap add ½ cup kerosene or coal oil. For disinfectant soap, add 1 teaspoonful of lysol. Add these ingredients when you add the lye.

For delicate perfumed hand soap add to the original ingredients:

    1 cup melted fat
    2 ounces lanolin
    3 ounces glycerine
    3 tablespoons finely ground oatmeal
    ⅓ cup sugar
    4 teaspoons aromatic Rose Geranium
    Strawberry shade dye (sold at drug stores by the ounce)

Add the sugar as you dissolve the lye. Mix in the other additional ingredients while adding the fat.

Soap-Making as an Art

Soap-making can be a creative art. For instance, you can

— Use molds of various sizes and shapes.

— Make a design on the top of the soap with pin pricks.

— Carve the soap when it has hardened.

— Wrap it in net and sequins for a gift.

CHAPTER 13

Outdoor Survival

Outdoor Cooking

People have cooked food in ages past without either electricity or gas, without pots or pans. It isn't too difficult to do today. Trying it out is fun and will make one feel more secure should an emergency arise. Here are some of the mediums you can use:

Clay. Cover a small animal or fish with stiff, moist clay about one inch thick. Bake in hot ashes. The clay will come away easily.

Leaves. Bake biscuits between *several* layers of sweet green leaves placed on hot ground and covered with ashes and hot coals.

Pit. Dig a pit big enough to hold a whole beef or small enough for a bird. Barbecue the animal in it.

Reflector oven. Anything shiny in front of a fire will reflect heat rays and thus will hasten cooking. Directions for making a metal reflector oven that weighs only 15 oz. and fits into an envelope are contained in the readily available book, *Fieldbook for Men and Boys*, published by Boy Scouts of America. A reflector oven can be improvised from a five-gallon can or from aluminum foil and sticks patterned after the one in the Scout handbook.

Rocks. Mankind has found uses for rocks in cooking since time began. The aborigines of Australia cooked kangaroos by filling their bodies with hot rocks. Boy Scouts today put red hot stones in the cavity of a chicken, wrap it in foil and a plastic bag, then drop it in a pack sack with dry leaves added for insulation. They take off in a canoe or up a trail, and in three or four hours a delicious chicken meal is ready for them. For other ideas, try

— Using a hole in the ground to cook soup. Line the hole with fresh hide or anything that will hold liquid. Drop clean pebbles in the bottom, then add some hot stones. Pour the soup over the hot stones, cover the hide, and the soup will cook.

— Using hollow rocks or shells for containers. Build a fire around them to heat water or soup.

— Steam cooking your meal. Lay food between layers of damp grass, then put this on hot stones you have put into a hole. Cover the top layer of grass with earth, and make a hole down through the layers with a stick, pouring water through this hole onto the hot stones as necessary. (Don't heat rocks just taken from a cold stream, as they will explode.)

— Making a Polynesian-style imu. Heat a stone-lined pit red hot, then rake out the fuel. On a thick layer of moistened sweet leaves put chicken, unhusked corn, sweet potatoes, whole pineapple. Cover with moist leaves, a wet burlap bag, and earth. After about two hours the food will be ready for a luau.

Sticks and wood

— String a line of little fish or frogs on a stick and cook them over hot coals.

— Run a peeled stick through a chicken and use it as a spit.

— Make a shish kebab by taking a two-foot straight stick about the diameter of a pencil, threading it alternately through small slices of meat and vegetables, and broiling the food over hot coals.

— Put a tiny stick through an egg, and turn it over hot coals for about 10 minutes.

— Preheat a peeled club of sweet wood about two inches thick, wet it, and twist a long "sausage" of dough around it. Turn it over hot coals to brown the dough evenly.

— Peg food on preheated hardwood slabs. Lean the slabs in front of a bank of glowing coals to cook the food.

*Reflector Oven, Stick, and Rock Surface Used to Bake
Dough Out of Doors*

Foil

— Assemble a hamburger pattie, onion slices, with potato and carrot slices on top. Make a neat, ash-proof package of them by wrapping them all in a 12-inch square of tinfoil. Seal the package securely and bake in hot ashes.

— In the same manner, try baking in hot ashes eggs, apples, or biscuits with berries.

Sun and wind

— Cut chunks of meat into thin strips. String them and hang them up for the sun and wind to dry. (It takes five pounds of fresh meat to make one pound dried.) Dried meat packed in fat will last a long time and is called "pemmican."

— Peel back corn husks and hang the corn by the husks, Indian fashion.

— Dry wild blackberries on the roof, on hot rocks, or in a home food dryer. (They taste like currants.)

Camp Life Ideas

Construct a *cooler* frame as big as a refrigerator or as small as a five-gallon can. Use burlap for the sides. Capillary action keeps the burlap wet and cool if you place the ends in a pan of water on the top of the cooler.

For a *wash basin*, light a fire in the cavity of a large rock. Scoop out the hot ashes and pour water in to produce heat. Soak your tired feet, or let the youngsters splash and play.

For *heat retention*, remember that your own body is a good "heater" (98.4° hot). Concentrate on ways to keep your body heat in. Keeping your head warm will help to do this.

For *containers* make use of

— "Skin bags" made of animal intestines or stomachs (I prefer plastic).

— A pit in the flour in the top of the sack, and mix the dough there.

— Half an orange skin to poach eggs in over coals.

— Shells or leaves to serve food on.

For free *fuel*, try

— Newspaper rolled tightly.

— Roots from small brush.

— Leftover fat.

— Rubber tires.

— Dried bark or animal dung.

Charcoal is another useful fuel. It can be made from twigs and limbs of fruit, nut, and other hardwood trees, from black walnuts or peach and apricot pits. It makes a hot fire which gives off little or no smoke.

To make charcoal, put the material in a can which has a few holes punched in it, put a lid on the can and "cook" the material over a hot fire. The holes in the can will allow the gases and flame to escape. The exclusion of oxygen keeps the material from completely burning up to ashes. When the flame from the holes in the can turns to yellow-red, remove the can from the fire.

Emergency equipment. If you are in a situation where there is a possibility of getting lost, it would be wise to have with you

— Matches, rifle, sharp knife, whistle, a rope and a sling.

— Two compasses, field glasses, and a two-way mirror (to attract attention if lost).

— Water-purifying tablets.[1]

Nature's Food Bargains

Nature provides free food to those who come to her store. The doors are open twenty-four hours a day, seven days a week.

---

[1]Information for outdoor cooking and camplife ideas was obtained from two fine books —*Fieldbook for Boys and Men*, Boy Scouts of America (New Brunswick, New Jersey No. 3201) and *Outdoor Survival* by Larry Dean Olson (University Press, Brigham Young University, Provo, Utah). Also, from countless family camp experiences.

Her list of edible plants numbers 120,000. How many have you tried?

If the markets should ever be out of food, if your pay check is slim, if you're feeling under par or if you just want an adventure in eating, try some of the following:

Tubers and Roots

    Cattail roots
    Camas bulbs
    Sego lily roots
    Wild onions
    Wappato tubers

Seeds

    Apple, pear or grape
    Chia (salvia columbariae)
    Lamb's-quarters (similar
      to caraway seed)
    Millet
    Sesame
    Sunflower
    Watermelon seed

Leaves (will relieve hunger)

    Apple leaves (bitter)
    Birch
    Chokecherry (sour)
    Elm (neutral taste)
    Maple (sour, then sweet)
    Poplar (bitter)

Wild Fruit

    Blackberries
    Blueberries
    Blue elderberries
    Salmonberries
    Thimbleberries
    Cherries
    Huckleberries

Greens (free vitamins and minerals)

    Cattail tip and lower six
      inches of leaf
    Chicory
    Fern tops (before they unroll)
    Horsetail tips (joint grass)
    Lamb's-quarters (pig weeds)
    Nasturtium leaves (peppery,
      good on sandwiches)
    Purslane
    Sorrel
    Thistle greens
    Watercress (appetizing)
    Wild asparagus

Other Foods Nature Supplies

    Pine nuts
    Wild honeycomb
    Syrup from birch trees
    Pollen for flour
    Seaweeds
    Fungi (relished by French and
      Italians)

Nutritious Tea

    Alfalfa and mint leaves
    Steeped evergreen needles
    Linden blossom tea
    Sage (Chinese drink this)
    Raspberry leaves

Hot Dark Brew

  Roast and grind:
    Wheat
    Barley
    Grated potatoes
    Dandelion roots
    Carob (locust bean) —
      for a cocoa-flavored
      drink

My Garden Drug Store

  Catnip tea — for babies with
    colic

Comfrey — for poultices
Garden sage — for hair rinse
Plantain leaf—for insect bites
Yarrow — for quinine substi-
  tute
Rose hips — for vitamin C
Hops — for inducing sleep

Eat it All

Carrots and tops
Turnip and beet greens
Broccoli stems, cabbage cores

CHAPTER 14

Care of the Body

It is not intended that this chapter give exhaustive information on the care and cure of the body. Rather it offers a few simple but not always obvious suggestions which will make for better general health, or for relief from pain under certain circumstances.

In talking to people I often sense that they are afraid of ill health and fearful of being without a doctor, especially in survival situations. It is true that today most of us can and do consult a physician when illness strikes. But this book is not written with normal times in mind. Should we ever be in a situation in which a doctor's aid is unobtainable, a basic understanding of how the body functions will at least help us in the first part of the problem — figuring out what we are trying to accomplish in treating an illness at home. The human body was created with such faculties and powers that it can miraculously maintain itself with very little assistance. By discovering something of how our body works we can develop the necessary faith and "know-how" to assist the body in its task of keeping in good working order.

I feel strongly that God intended his children to be well in mind and body. Yet a recent report from the Public Health Service states that 74 million people in the United States are chronically ill, and four million are so ill that they can't work.

We should be thankful that doctors can provide us with a mechanical hand or heart, a metal leg shaft or a movable knee joint if we should need it, as well as supplying many other services and treatments the rest of us are not qualified to handle. But considering all the advantages we have in modern life, it seems that more of the responsibility for keeping well should rest on the individual's shoulders. This would be especially important in survival conditions.

How the Body Works

Cells. Cells are tiny units found in all living things. In our bodies their shapes resemble bricks, plates, ribbons, and spirals. (A nerve cell may have a tail several feet long.) We have "fixed" cells in bones, muscles, etc., and mobile ones in the blood. No matter what their shape or size, they all have to be nourished.

The health of the cell depends on the quality of the blood bringing food nutrients and oxygen and taking away impurities. Healthy blood = healthy cells = healthy parts of the body. Blood quality can be improved by proper nutrition and water intake, and by fresh air and sunshine.

Skin. It takes about 18 square feet of skin to cover the body. Skin is porous, and it absorbs as well as eliminates (through hair shafts, oil glands, and sweat gland tubes that rise to the surface). Certain chemicals placed on the skin can be tasted twenty minutes later. Oxygen is absorbed through the skin. Nerve endings and other apparatus near the skin sense pain, pressure, heat and cold. Yards of blood vessels are near the surface of the skin.

There is much one can do to assist the skin in doing its work. For example: improving one's general health; keeping the skin clean; opening and closing the pores by exercise, hot baths, and cold showers.

Bones. Bones are composed of 20 percent liquid, the solids comprising $\frac{2}{3}$ calcium, phosphorus, etc., and $\frac{1}{3}$ organic matter (a protein fiber). Both the minerals and the protein are needed for strong bones (like bricks and mortar in a building). Red blood cells are developed from the red marrow. They are produced in the spongy area of the long bones, and in the ribs and vertebrae.

Muscles. Muscles make up more than half the weight of the human body. They resemble a bunch of rubber bands bound tightly together. Exercise increases the elasticity and weight of muscles. We can learn to control some of our involuntary muscles.

Brain. The brain is a broadcasting and receiving set. Each person has both a conscious and a subconscious mind, and he can exercise control over his thoughts in both these areas. Using the right techniques and controls we can get thoughts into and out of the subconscious mind, and thus help in accomplishing our goals in life. A formula for accomplishment would be:

$$G + P + M + R + F = A$$

where G is a goal, P is a plan to achieve it, M is correct motivation, R is repetition (necessary to impress the other factors on the subconscious mind), F is faith, and A is achievement.

Nerves. The nervous system is like a telephone system — it can receive and send messages. One kind of nerve carries impulses on their way to the brain, another carries command impulses from the brain to the muscles.

Senses. The normal person can see, hear, touch, smell and taste; and he can sense pressure, heat, cold and pain.

Digestive system. The adult digestive system is over 30 feet long. In it the food we eat is chemically broken down into liquids which can seep into the blood stream through the thread-like villi in the small intestine. The breaking-down process is carried out by juices — first the juices from the salivary glands in the mouth, then the stronger gastric juices in the stomach. Gall bladder, liver, pancreas, and the intestine walls themselves all drip digestive juices over the semi-liquid food mass as it leaves the churning stomach and takes its place in the wave-like contractions of the small intestine.

The more solid undigested fibers, seeds, skins, etc., move into the large intestine and wait there in the "terminal" to be expelled.

Circulation. The heart is a muscle organ which pumps the blood around the body. As with other muscles, proper exercise and nourishment produce strong heart muscles. Nerves regulate the heart's activities. A tense body interferes with blood circulation.

Circulation can be increased by removing congestion in lungs, skin, kidneys, liver and bowels — five organs or areas that eliminate impurities caused by dead cells, which are toxic. If one of these is not functioning properly it is wise to help activate the others.

Respiration. Oxygen enters the blood through the air we breathe into our lungs, and carbon dioxide (a waste product) passes out through the lungs in like manner. We can improve the oxygen intake if we breathe deeply, breathe cool air, and live where there is green vegetation.

Body cells need oxygen to provide the spark necessary for combustion, so that the nourishment in the cells can be burned and provide us with energy for body movements. Red corpuscles carry the oxygen to the cells.

The respiratory cavities (nose, etc.) leading to the outside of the body are lined with a thin coating of mucus that traps germs and dust, thus helping to keep these away from the lungs. Anything that dries out the lining of the throat or nose or bronchial tubes may cause a person to cough. Fevers dry out the lining of the throat; so does breathing through the mouth, which in children is often caused by large adenoids.

At the front of the throat is the windpipe, which leads into the lung cavity. At the back of the throat is the esophagus, which connects with the stomach. Occasionally a person chokes on something. Slapping him hard on the back is dangerous — he gasps, and the inrush of air may be such that the object is drawn into the windpipe and goes down the bronchial tube. The solution is rather to keep relaxed, and the object can then usually be coughed up.

Liquid excretion. Water helps the body to dissolve food nutrients and carry them along to the cells. It also helps to dissolve waste products within the cells so that the blood can carry them away. The body has a high water content — if you weigh 90 lb., about 60 lb. of this is water.

Liquid waste products pass through the kidneys into the bladder. Each kidney contains millions of tiny coiled tubes, through which blood flows. The liver converts amino acids to sugar and ammonia, which is converted to urea and passes out of the system through the kidneys and bladder as urine.

In older women, inability to control urine flow may be due to poor muscle tone (or scar tissue from infection) of the small opening of the bladder.

Emotions. We all have approximately the same emotional needs — such as being loved, feeling important, and having new experiences. For many, including myself, there is a conscious need for a close relationship with God. Attempts to satisfy emotional needs explain many of our actions.

The spotlight today seems to be on emotionally induced illness. Fear, indecision, and negative thoughts make the body tense and restrict the flow of blood that nourishes the cells. This in turn reduces the body's ability to fight off germs. After consuming germs, white blood cells need good blood circulation in order to be rapidly carried away and replaced by others which will repeat the process.

Our emotions are often reflected in the skin. Tension may cause wet palms, red nose, perspiring, or blushing. It may make acne and other skin disorders get worse.

Care of the Skin

Under a magnifying glass, skin shows ridges and valleys containing open pores and hair shafts. Fungus, dirt (blackheads), parasites and bacteria find these ideal places in which to lodge and multiply, especially in out-of-the-way places where it is warm and moist — like between toes, back of ears, and under fingernails.

For skin-soothers, use corn starch, baking soda, vaseline, and oils.

Minor Ailments and Emergencies

Fever. Fever is one of Nature's ways of helping the body destroy germs, virus and toxins. But while elevated temperatures serve a purpose, control is necessary to prevent the burning of cells and tissues, especially in the brain.

A temperature above the normal of 98.4° is a sign that something is out of order — infection, inflammation, etc. A temperature in a child usually rises more rapidly than in adults, but it also subsides quicker. A temperature of 103° in a child is no more serious than one of 102° in an adult. (Rectal temperature is one degree higher than mouth temperature.)

Symptoms of a fever are as follows: Flushed face; underarm warmth; hot dry skin; headache; all-over body ache; scant, highly-colored urine; vomiting; constipation or diarrhea; cold feet; increased pulse rate; rapid breathing; chills and shivering alternating with hot flushes. Fever sores sometimes develop.

To treat a fever

— Put the person to bed.

— For fever of more than 103° by mouth in children, cool the body by sponging it with cool water or rubbing alcohol. Put an ice bag or cold compress on the head. Change this as often as the skin becomes heated.

— Give plenty of liquids. (Lemon juice in water quenches thirst and helps to destroy germs.)

— Keep the patient in bed until the fever has been normal for 24 hours. (Aspirin will reduce fever and help to relieve aches and pains.)

Chest congestion. Mustard plasters are a good remedy for congestion in the chest. Mix 1 egg, 1 tablespoon of dry mustard and 2 tablespoons of lard; thicken with flour, spread the mixture on thin cloth and put this between flannel. Apply it to the chest.

Coughs. To lubricate and sooth irritated membranes there are countless preparations on the market. For a home remedy try honey as a base, using equal parts either of honey and butter or honey and lemon juice. Another possibility: Combine ½ cup of honey, a grated onion and ½ cup of water, and simmer for 15 minutes. Strain while hot. Give one teaspoon as dose, and repeat dosage as necessary.

Digestive problems. Occasionally trouble arises along the digestive route. As preventive measures you should

— Relax, give thanks, and serve food attractively. This will encourage better flow of digestive juices.

— Improve general body health: glands secrete juices; nerves (from the spine) regulate the motion of the intestines; muscle tone affects the movement of food through muscular organs of esophagus, stomach and intestines.

— Find and use food combinations which are best for you. Personally I prefer using vegetables for the main meal and adding either protein or carbohydrates, with not much liquids or milk at mealtime. Lactic acid in foods helps prevent putrefaction in the intestines.

You can break up a compact food mass and move it along by

— Good lubrication — oils from nuts, soy beans and grains, cream, butter, and avocados. Onions contain oil.

— Including in the diet the right amount of bulky foods (vegetables, whole grains, etc.).

— Eating fresh and dried fruit — the sugars here cause a gas that breaks up a food mass.

— Drinking water and fruit juices.

Diarrhea. Infants are more susceptible than adults to diarrhea. The cause may be polluted water, milk or other foods, or germs from human waste (spread by hands or flies).

Diarrhea is Nature's way of getting rid of poisons or substances that do not agree with the body. It draws moisture from tissues, and brings the danger of dehydration. It is important to restore the fluids lost by this means.

Childbirth. The prospect of a baby being born without a doctor seems like reason for panic until you've gone through the experience. My fifth baby was born unexpectedly at home on a beautiful Easter morning. The doctor arrived to take care of the afterbirth and tie the cord. (No hurry! A story is told of a mother walking for miles with her baby to have the cord tied.)

Miscarriage. To retard bleeding during symptoms of miscarriage, lie flat on the bed with the foot of the bed elevated 12 to 18 inches. Put an ice bag on the stomach, keep warm and quiet, and drink liquids. Vitamin K may prevent excessive bleeding.

Water Treatments

Water can be a simple, effective, safe treatment. It is used both internally and externally and costs almost nothing.

Books on water therapy were being written five hundred years before the time of Christ. Ancient peoples knew the value of their luxury baths. One historian says that the absence of bathing during the dark ages in Europe, when the bath was unknown, accounted for the plagues and pestilences of that period.

Today we are still using water to help take care of our bodies. We use ice, steam, hot and cold packs, and baths.

Ice. Ice has many uses. For relieving pain

— Hold burned fingers in a bowl of cold water containing ice cubes. If this is begun within thirty seconds from the time of the burn, it will arrest the continuing burning process that damages tissues.

— Before lancing a boil, removing a sliver, or giving an injection, first freeze the skin with an ice cube.

— First apply an ice pack to sprains on any part of the body. (After 24 to 48 hours move the joint as much as possible, using hot packs to increase blood circulation.)

For reducing infection, hold ice on a wound until it can be dressed. This helps to keep germs dormant, just as we refrigerate food to keep germs from multiplying.

For restricting bleeding

— Hold ice over a wound with pressure applied, thus constricting the blood vessels until clotting takes place.

— Use ice to prevent internal bleeding from bumps or bruises (black-and-blue discoloration from torn blood vessels).

For other uses

—Apply ice to relieve itching caused by bites or rash.

— Rub ice over the face and neck to help prevent a person from fainting from heat.

Steam. Steam inhalations are used to relieve croup, nasal congestion, coughs, or loss of voice. Today we use moist cold vapor (55°) from an inhalator, instead of the hot steam from a teakettle.

Hot and cold packs. Hot and cold packs give relief from pain, stiffness or infection. This is because they increase blood circulation, which is beneficial because

— It brings more food nutrients and oxygen to the cells.

— It carries away toxic wastes from dying cells.

— It brings more germ-devouring white corpuscles to the scene of the trouble.

There are three types of packs:

1. Alternate hot and cold (30 seconds cold, 3 minutes hot, beginning and ending with cold): This is useful in either drawing infection to the surface as with a boil, or dispersing it into the system, as with a swollen neck gland (if treated in time) to prevent lancing.

2. Hot pack: This will relieve a backache. On the back put a wet bath towel, folded in thirds, as hot as the person can stand. Leave it for 20 minutes at a time. A heat lamp, hot water bottle or heating pad over the wet towel will keep it hot. (Moist heat is always more effective than dry for this purpose, and is less likely to burn the skin.) Repeat in about 40 minutes.

3. Warming compress: This is used for convenience during the night. It is an ice-cold wet cloth covered with a wool cloth, and it produces the same effect of vasodilatation as hot and cold packs.

The preparation of a warming compress depends on the location of the pain or infection.

— For a *sore throat*, use a piece of muslin 4 inches wide and long enough to go around the neck twice. Dip it in ice water, press it out with one hand, put it around the neck and cover it with a wool cloth.

— For *pain in finger joints*, put on a cloth glove soaked in ice water and pressed out, and cover it with a wool glove.

— For *pain in feet and ankles*, similarly use a wet cotton sock and cover it with a wool sock.

In some instances, repeated treatment over a lengthy period may be necessary.

Baths — hot and cold. We take baths for at least three reasons — to clean the skin, to help eliminate toxins, and to stimulate and activate the skin.

We clean the skin to remove poisons from perspiration left on it which inhibit the ability of the pores to breathe and eliminate waste.

We take hot baths to help eliminate toxins through the sweat glands. Perspiration can be induced by adding to the water skin-irritants such as mustard, sage, thyme, elderberry leaves, and the commonly-used epsom salt. Add three cups of epsom salt to a half tub of hot water. Begin with 98° and increase to 104° and above. Remain in the bath for about 20 minutes. The pulse may increase from 70 to 150. Drink water before and after the bath. Put a cold cloth on the head, and use caution in getting out of the tub if you feel faint. Warm baths relax nerves and induce sleep.

A cold shower or rub down activates the skin and makes the body less susceptible to changes in temperatures.

A hot sitz bath or hip bath is used to relieve itching piles.

We use water for many other purposes such as

— For washing a wound (plain soap and water is considered a good antiseptic).

— For an eye wash (add one teaspoon of salt to one quart of water).

— For increasing the blood circulation in the region of the eyes by splashing warm water on them.

PART IV

A FUTURE
OF HOPE

CHAPTER 15

New Era Market

Come with me on a tour of a future food center, a store which portrays a new concept in marketing and human relations. If the ideas seem fanciful, even fantastic, remember that a lot of ideas which were once given those labels are now accepted practices. Meanwhile one can hope.

Place to relax. First let's visit "Ye Olde Mill." Relax a moment as you watch the old water wheel turn and splash in a clear pond. Inside the mill, automatic stone burr mills grind away and feed the products into a wall vending-machine type of installation. On view back of clear glass are the grains and seeds and nuts. By pressing a selector button on the vending machine one releases a package of either whole, coarse grind or fine grind products, or any combination of grinds desired.

Garden shop. The nostalgia for the peaceful country returns as you view murals picturing green watercress growing along the bank of a meandering stream. Seen through the windows, bushels of red tomatoes, green garden rows, fruit trees in blossom, yellow pumpkin, and fields of waving corn gladden the heart. Inside, portable counter-height vats of growing greens and trays of sprouting seeds and grains insure maximum freshness for this kind of produce. All produce has a label of guarantee — it was grown on soil organically fertilized. Flats or pots of parsley, chives, etc., are available to take home and transplant in a window box or in small pots. Seed packets also are offered.

Measured Meal Department. Here you can pick up a package of measured meals for the day containing any calorie count desired. You can get either a protein or a carbohydrate meal, properly balanced. These are not space age rations, but ordinary fresh food.

Midday pickup. Here is a finger-food snack bar, offering fresh vegetables, whole fruit or juices. Before the snack, fill your lungs with fresh air in compartments available for that purpose, or relax and meditate on a cot in a sound-proof booth, or use a vibrating chair or hand vibrator. The choice is yours.

Health Center. A qualified consultant is on duty at all times to suggest fresh foods, growing plants and herbs as remedies for minor ailments and discomforts.

Storage foods. Instead of canned vegetables, there are fermented foods in glass bottles with glass lids — raw uncooked string beans, sauerkraut, beets, pickles, turnips, etc. All have shelf lives of over two years.

Festival fancies. For special occasions there are fancy foods to add zest and variety and spark up the common grains and produce of everyday fare. Here are beasts of the field and fowl of the air, deliciously precooked to order. On display too are sweets and all the delicacies, tempting and appealing to the eye and taste — all for your use and delight on *special occasions.*

Financing. The market is financed under a cooperative membership agreement — members pay in advance for their year's supply of food and services. There is no need for advertising, and no price signs mar the quiet atmosphere and beauty of the display and shopping area.

Inviting atmosphere. Shopping in this atmosphere of soft pleasant music, breathing air filled with the fragrance of growing things, observing healthy people who are fair in face and form and who exemplify the motto, "Eat to live, not live to eat" — this kind of shopping is a great advance on the rush and bustle and frustration of weekend marketing. No need to tell us to hurry back. We will!

CHAPTER 16

Live to Be a Hundred

My friends often kid me about living to be a hundred. Even assuming that I were certain of doing this, merely keeping alive isn't enough for me. I have to be alive and *well.* I might want to climb a mountain when I'm 99 and see what's over the top.

I've read many books on health. All the different opinions on how to keep well make me think of a big nutrition pot being stirred vigorously by many hands. Since I'm not an expert, maybe I should pull my ladle out and wait for more qualified people to taste and test and have mechanical brains process the data.

But expert or not, with information and experience I've gathered up here and there I've mixed up a brew. With the correct daily doses I think you and I could live to be a hundred. As my personal prescription for health and longevity I intend to

— Eat more green and root vegetables, mostly raw.

— Eat less in quantity.

— Get more exercise.

— Ensure good elimination.

— Cultivate peace of mind and emotional control.

With the idea of fortifying my will, and perhaps of encouraging others, I here set out some of my reasons and express my resolve for the future.

Raw foods. I'm responsible for the nourishment of 40 trillion living cells in my body. I think they would do better on live raw foods. This conclusion is based not merely on reading but on my observations of others and on my own experience. I feel better with an abundance of raw foods in my diet.

Foods seldom eaten raw that really taste good that way are: asparagus, beets, broccoli, endive, mushrooms, parsley, peas, potatoes, spinach and turnips. Vegetables contain more minerals than fruits do, and are of more value to the body. For more robust, vigorous health I'm resolving to eat more uncooked foods.

Eat less, feel best. The quantity of food we need depends on factors such as age, occupation, metabolism, and even on attitude toward life. Most Americans eat too much. Personally I'm going to eat less because I know I can do so healthfully and because the last family reunion picture makes me look as if I need to. My body has to handle every shipment of food it receives. Over the next 45 years, if it consistently gets more than it can use, the machinery may wear out and then I won't live to be a hundred. I have heard it said that half of what we eat keeps us alive and the other half kills us, and I can well believe it.

Some food combinations I like best are

— Vegetables with virtually all foods.

— Leafy green vegetables with protein.

— Lunch of fruit with nuts, cheese, milk or eggs.

— Protein sandwich fillings in celery, on apple slices, or rolled in a cabbage leaf.

— Warm whole wheat bread with fresh picked parsley or with sliced tomatoes, radishes, lettuce or green onions.

— Sweet dried fruit fillings and wheat thins.

— Meat with raw cranberries and orange sauce.

— Wheat, milk, honey and salt — for an emergency.

Exercise. I'm going to take regular exercise and breathe deeply

— To keep the five quarts of blood in my veins and arteries on the move.

— To provide every cell with an "electrical" spark from oxygen, which is needed to provide the combustion which will completely burn up food nutrients.

— To facilitate the expulsion of carbon dioxide and other wastes.

— To maintain proper body weight.

— To have firm muscles for more attractive appearance, and to have supple, free-wheeling joints and limbs.

All kinds of exercise are available. If I don't feel like jogging, I can try isometric exercises, by which muscles of the whole body can be strengthened while lying in bed. Karate and yoga are popular now. I like to swim. I've been reading about heart trouble and am impressed by the claims that physically active people seldom have it.

Internal traffic. It is easy to have a traffic tie-up somewhere along the intestinal tunnel, which is as long as my front room (24 feet), varies in diameter, and abounds in loops and kinks. I think it is my individual responsibility to maintain a free flow of traffic in this tunnel.

Personal hygiene is important to me inside as well as outside my body. Elimination of body wastes is essential to health. Death through retention of waste poisons comes faster than that resulting from starvation. For better elimination there are many recommendations: more fats, more roughage, better muscle tone, regular habits, massage, exercise. Liquids are important. Water dissolves waste products within the cells and also dissolves food materials in the blood so that they can pass through membranes to cells.

Peace of mind and emotional control. In aspiring to live to a hundred, emotional balance should be the first consideration. My reading convinces me that chronic disease starts with toxins in the blood which often are partly the result of a tense body and a mind full of fear, worry, anxiety, and self-pity. This wrong mental and spiritual attitude to life is as much to blame for poor health as wrong food, stimulants and over-eating. For it is not what we eat but what we digest and assimilate that is of value to our bodies.

Life is meant to be lived in a positive, affirmative manner, with a confident but calm reaching for the truly best things life offers. To live this way is not only to encourage and attract the factors which make for happy, satisfying living but also to promote healthful body processes.

A course I took encouraged the students to set down in writing what each wanted in life, what he was willing to give in return, and how and when he proposed to achieve the goals concerned.[1] Carrying out this plan gave me a feeling of having a strong support at my back. From now until I'm a hundred, if I put into practice all I've learned I'll have more of many things — things like peace of mind, love, resilience, and even the bounties of this life. And along the way my health can't fail to profit.

The simple things that make life happy also make it healthy, and vice versa. Plant a garden — even if it's a small one. It will gladden your heart as it does mine to pick fresh vegetables in the summer. Plant seven greens which are high in the vitamins and minerals important for immunity to disease, good nerves, and overall vitality: beet greens, mustard greens, parsley, spinach, Swiss chard, turnip greens, and watercress. Plant them close together in little beds. In the winter eat sprouts from seeds and grains, and plant parsley and chives in indoor pots. I bought a tiny coffee grinder which I hold between my knees and use to grind grains and seeds. It grinds coarse or powder-fine. It is about as efficient as the saddlestones of 3000 B.C., but it's fun and it really works.

Restful, restorative sleep is a big part of happy, healthful living. When friends come to visit at my home we let them have our beautiful bedroom that otherwise stands empty. We're sleeping outside for the rest of our lives and we know that we don't have to sleep as long outside as indoors in order to feel rested — in fact the sleeping patio is the best feature of our new home. My family slept outside for eight years in California. There is a great joy in waking up to see the sky and the clouds and to listen to the song of a meadowlark. The moon and stars are so beautiful that I just want to stay awake at night watching them.

Moving closer to Nature's beauties is one way I seek peace of mind and emotional stability. I might add that it increases my feeling of closeness to God who created it and who is the primary source of my happiness in life.

[1]*Science of Personal Achievement* by Napoleon Hill, author of *Think and Grow Rich.*

CHAPTER 17

Brighter Day

The previous chapter's mention of peace of mind and emotional stability leads naturally into the theme of this chapter — a brighter day. In every country our generation is beset by a multitude of problems which promise to bequeath even worse ones to the succeeding generation, all threatening to peace and happiness. Where is the brighter day?

I am one who believes that that day will come, but there may first be worse times for this world than we have yet seen. While the advice given in this book is good for other circumstances too, it is written principally with this premise in mind and with the idea of encouraging preparation for survival in the event of such trying times.

Man Could Solve His Problems

Ironically, while multiplying his problems man has in his grasp the tools for a better, more abundant life. For instance, in the matter of food supply for a burgeoning world population, and in spite of the dire predictions and the frightening statistics we read, scientists, engineers, technicians and others have joined forces to solve the problem of hunger. Many solutions are already a reality and more are on the way. Here are a few of the partial solutions, which embrace both suggestions for better organization of available resources and some of the modern miracles already accomplished.

1. Better distribution of food.

2. Improvement of yield. Not long ago an organic fertilizer from a quartz mine in Utah tripled production for a California tomato grower.

3. New high-production foods. Canada has a new "man-made" grain called "triticale" which produces 55 bushels to the acre and contains 4% more protein than wheat.[1]

---

[1]Noel Grove, "Science to the Rescue — Man-made Grain Showing Promise," *Oregon Journal*, June 21, 1967.

4. Hydrophonics.

The growing of plants in nutrient solutions — makes possible many - storied factories growing trays of vegetables and grains.

5. Addition of new areas to cultivation.

At the present time only 7% of the total land mass on our globe permits normal agriculture.

6. Foods growing in colder lands.

The Russians have developed a hybridized wheat that will ripen in shorter northern summers. New applications of genetic principles can add new varieties and open up new production areas.

7. Treated salt water for irrigation.

New de-salination processes are being perfected. Present means produce 1,000 gallons of useful water for 30¢, too expensive for agricultural use.

8. Plankton (sea plants and animals) for human consumption.

Plankton forms the base of the food pyramid in the complex chain of life in the sea. Since it is as high as 70% protein and 15% fat, it would be an excellent source of food. At present, it is less expensive to catch fish that eat plankton than to process the plankton for human consumption.

9. Better utilization of sea products.

A fish protein concentrate (FPC) has been developed which utilizes some of the less commercial species of sea life.

10. Synthesized combinations.

Example: nutrients such as algae flavored with pork and beef.

11. Production and perfection of an all-vegetable milk.

The world's food supply is just one of the many common problems of our age wherein team effort and cooperative group action can produce workable solutions. Clearly the world has, or can readily develop, the know-how for such solutions.

But the difficulty is not so much "know-how" as "do-how." National and international tensions and anxieties, and mutually exclusive ideologies, seem to preclude the cooperation necessary to solve world problems. Yet health and happiness require an optimistic, positive view of life. How can one maintain this attitude in the discouraging modern context?

Good Reasons for Optimism

Since this book has in large measure recorded my personal experiences and observations, let me here give my own views and convictions on this important subject. They spring from my faith in God and in the scriptures, and they center around the blueprint for living given by the Savior, Jesus Christ, two thousand years ago. Anyone who will take the time to study this blueprint can know the answers to the world's problems and by applying the answers in his own life can make his contribution to the larger solutions.

For me, life must have a clearly defined purpose — we must take our opportunities seriously and make our contributions meaningful. It is God who gives meaning to life. It is his Spirit which helps me and many others to face each new day with courage and optimism. As mankind try to live the great eternal laws of the universe and allow the power of God to work through them, science and technology will serve the purposes of both God and man in giving us the physical environment for a heaven on earth. But this miracle would be empty and barren without the greater one— the change that needs to take place in the hearts of men so that the Master's blueprint will be brought to fruition.

I believe that America is a nation with a prophetic mission to fulfill. Its discovery, colonization, revolution and constitutional structure were all under the influence of divine guidance. It was designed to be a great and free nation. Its history has been a reflection of its role as a beacon light to the world, a refuge and a promised land, a Christian nation. It was intended never to be destroyed, so long as its people would obey God's commandments.

Further Decline Before Brighter Day

Unfortunately every nation seems to be getting progressively more disobedient to the will of God. Many scriptural references indicate that the downward spiral, both morally and socially, will continue until a new day dawns with the second coming of Jesus Christ, the "Prince of Peace." The evil influences that are abroad in the world today, filling men's hearts with discord and contention, will at that time be eradicated. With the coming of the "Brighter Day," wars will end and peace and happiness will exist for all of God's children who remain on earth.

Many changes will take place as we move toward the "Brighter Day." Winston Churchill said, "The Stone Age may return on the gleaming wings of science," and well it might. The affluent American way of life could be interrupted. If this happens, our mental and physical well-being will depend on how well we are prepared and how well we are conditioned to accept the change — probably in a time of chaos. Our standard of living will be in proportion to the preparation we have made to be independent and to provide for our own and our family's daily necessities. A big factor in it all will be our mental and spiritual outlook, our faith and our courage.

Faith in God Is the Key

For me, the great inspiration is faith in God. The Psalmist expressed it far better than I can, in the immortal 23rd Psalm:

> The Lord is my shepherd; I shall not want.
> He maketh me to lie down in green pastures:
> He leadeth me beside the still waters.
>
> He restoreth my soul:
> He leadeth me in the paths of righteousness
> For his name's sake.
>
> Yea, though I walk though the valley of the
>   shadow of death,
> I will fear no evil;
> For thou art with me;
> Thy rod and thy staff they comfort me.

Thou preparest a table before me in the
   presence of mine enemies:
Thou anointest my head with oil;
My cup runneth over.

Surely goodness and mercy shall follow me
   all the days of my life:
And I will dwell in the house of the Lord forever.

And the Savior himself issued the divine invitation and promise:

Come unto me, all ye that labour and are heavy laden, and
I will give you rest.
Take my yoke upon you, and learn of me; for I am meek and
lowly in heart; and ye shall find rest unto your souls.
For my yoke is easy, and my burden is light.

(Matt. 11:28-30.)

Faith is not an abstract principle but an inspiration for living. It elevates the spirits, giving zest and vigor to daily life and imparting enthusiastic assurance for the future. Let me give briefly some of the thoughts about the future which fly on the wings of my faith.

In my mind's eye I see the radiance of the Brighter Day emerging from the cleansing fires which will eliminate the world's evils. I expect to hang on, to live to enjoy that day. I may even be living in the same house as now, looking east every day to enjoy the same rugged grandeur that is Mount Hood. There I see myself living, loving, laughing and sharing. There I want to continue to teach my children and their children the laws of health, respect for their bodies as the temples of God, and the joy of honest work.

As I walk with them we will talk of the sun, God's great gift that strengthens our bodies and grows our food. As we breathe deeply I will explain the reason why — why every body cell responds to air. As we cup our hands to drink from the rippling stream we will talk of the ways in which water helps us to be clean and well.

Together we will develop the gift for wonder as we marvel at sprouting seeds and green grass, at garden rows and ripening fruit. We will seek to understand the soil, and by our own labors we will keep it fertile. From our hearts we will be grateful for the "simple" things, like singing birds and the restored balance of Nature. And as the days go by we will all give and accept love in its many forms. We will have trust for one another. We will appreciate each other's worth.

Most important, in that brighter day on bended knees we will freely acknowledge God's great gifts and blessings and seek his guidance. For this is essentially what will make it the Brighter Day — when as children of God we apply his plan and accept his offer to walk beside us until we finish life's journey.

For me, then, faith in God engenders hope, which is part of the positive, optimistic way of life essential to true health and happiness. One who has this, and has made the necessary material preparations, can hope to survive any difficulties and calamities which may overtake the world before the Brighter Day emerges. And if he is called to leave this life before the testing time he will cheerfully accept this as God's will. Either way he will see his brighter day, whether in this life or in the next. Either way, too, he will know that he has tried to pass on to his loved ones the attitudes and practices which will equip them not merely for survival but for the ultimate achievement and enjoyment of their brighter day.

In the final analysis, what matters more than this?

CHAPTER 18

Survival Bookshelf

If your baggage is limited on your "survival expedition" (time of departure unknown) I suggest you take *Passport to Survival*. It will get you there all right. But it would be nice to have a few more books if circumstances permit. Here are my suggestions.

DIET AND HEALTH

Tobe, John H. *Guideposts to Health and Vigorous Long Life.* St. Catharines, Ontario, Canada: Modern Publications, 1967.

Kloss, Jethro. *Back to Eden.* Coalmont, Tennessee: Longview Publishing House, 1967 (15th printing).

Jarvis, D. C., M.D. *Folk Medicine.* New York: Henry Holt and Company, 1960 (17th printing).

Kordel, Lelord, Sc.D. *Eat and Grow Younger.* New York: Macfadden-Bartell Corporation, 1962. (205 East 42nd Street, New York, New York 10017.)

Pruden, Bonnie. *Physical Fitness.* New York: Ronald Publishing Company, 1959. (79 Madison Avenue, New York, New York 10016.)

Schifferes, Justus J., Ph.D. *Family Medical Encyclopedia.* New York: Perma Editions Affiliated Publishers, Inc. (630 Fifth Avenue, New York, New York 10020.)

Readers Digest Handbook of First Aid. New York: Readers Digest. (Pleasantville, New York.)

Widtsoe, John A. and Leah D. *The Word of Wisdom.* Salt Lake City, Utah: Deseret Book Co., 1950.

Cooper, Kenneth Hardy. *Aerobics.* Philadelphia: J. B. Lippincott Co., 1931. (East Washington Square, Philadelphia, Pennsylvania 19105.)

FOOD

Meal Preparation

Fathman, George and Doris. *Live Foods.* Tucson: Sun Haven Publishers, 1967. (Route 9, Box 968-A, Tucson, Arizona 85700.) (192 recipes—mostly uncooked foods.)

Hunter, Beatrice Trum. *The Natural Foods Cookbook.* New York: Pyramid Publications, Inc, 1967. (444 Madison Avenue, New York, New York 10022.)

Rosenvall, Miller and Flack. *Wheat for Man.* Salt Lake City, Utah: Bookcraft, Inc., 1966. (Whole wheat recipes.)

Davis, Adelle. *Let's Cook It Right.* New York: Harcourt Brace and Company, 1962. (757 Third Avenue, New York, New York 10017.)

Food Storage

Zabriskie, Bob R. *Family Storage Plan.* Salt Lake City, Utah: Bookcraft, Inc., 1966.

Egan, Merritt H., M.D. *Home Storage.* Salt Lake City, Utah: Welfare Department, The Church of Jesus Christ of Latter-day Saints, 1959.

Food Chemistry and Nutrition

Quigley, D. T., M.D., F.A.C.S. *The National Malnutrition.* Milwaukee: Lee Foundation for Nutritional Research, 1952. (2023 West Wisconsin Avenue, Milwaukee, Wis. 53200.)

Portfolio of Reprints for the Layman and Housewife. Milwaukee: Lee Foundation for Nutritional Research, June 1959. (2023 West Wisconsin Avenue, Milwaukee, Wis. 53200.) (62 reprints.)

Bailey, Herbert, and Fredericks, Carlton. *Food Facts and Fallacies.* New York: ARC Books, Inc., 1969. (219 Park Avenue South, New York, New York 10003.)

Elwood, Catharyn. *Feel Like a Million!* New York: Pocket Books, a division of Simon & Schuster, Inc., 1967. (1 West 39th Street, New York, New York 10018.)

Heinz Nutritional Data. Pittsburgh, Pennsylvania: H. J. Heinz Co., 1964. (P. O. Box 57, Pittsburgh, Pennsylvania.)

Heinz Handbook of Nutrition. New York: McGraw-Hill Book Co., 1965.

Bailey, Herbert. *Vitamin E Your Key to a Healthy Heart*. New York: ARC Books, Inc., 1967. (219 Park Avenue South, New York, New York 10003.)

Tilden, J. H., M.D. *Toxemia Explained*. Mokelumne Hill, California: Health Research, 1955.

Agriculture and World Food Supply

Paddock, William and Paul. *Famine 1975*. Boston, Massachusetts: Little Brown and Company, 1967.

Van Gorder, Dan P. *Ill Fares the Land*. Belmont, Massachusetts: Western Islands, 1966.

Carson, Rachel. *Silent Spring*. Greenwich, Connecticut: Fawcett Publications, Inc., 1962.

FALLOUT PROTECTION

Fallout Protection. Department of Defense, Office of Civil Defense. (Other Civil Defense publications are available from your local civil defense office without charge; or write to Jeffersonville Census Operations Office, 1201 East 10th St., Jeffersonville, Indiana 47130.)

POSITIVE, PROGRESSIVE LIVING

Fromm, Erich. *The Art of Loving*. New York: Harper Publishing Company, 1956.

Maltz, Maxwell, M.D., F.I.C.S. *Psycho-Cybernetics*. New York: Simon & Schuster, Inc., 1960.

Hill, Napoleon. *Think and Grow Rich*. New York: Hawthorne Books, 1966. (70 Fifth Ave., New York, New York 10000.)

Hill, Napoleon. *The Science of Personal Achievement*. Columbia, South Carolina: The Napoleon Hill Foundation Course, 1963. (P. O. Box 1721, Columbia, South Carolina 29200.)

OUTDOOR SURVIVAL

Olsen, Larry Dean. *Outdoor Survival Skills*. Provo, Utah: Brigham Young University Press.

Herter, George Leonard, and Jacques P. *Professional Guide's Manual*. Louisville, Kentucky: Fawcett-Haynes Printing Corporation, 1966. (Contains over 500 outdoor tips.)

Fieldbook for Boys and Men. New Brunswick, New Jersey: Boy Scouts of America, No. 3201.

PRESERVATION OF FREEDOM

Benson, Ezra Taft. *An Enemy Hath Done This.* Salt Lake City: Parliament Publishers, 1969. (1848 West 2300 South, Salt Lake City, Utah 84119.)

Weaver, Henry Grady. *Mainspring of Human Progress.* Irvington-on-Hudson, New York: Foundation for Economic Education, 1965.

Newquist, Jerreld L. *Prophets, Principles and National Survival.* Salt Lake City, Utah: Publishers Press, 1964. (1900 West 2300 South, Salt Lake City, Utah 84119.)

Andersen, H. Verlan. *Many Are Called but Few Are Chosen.* Provo: Press Publishing Company, 1967. (175 West First North, Provo, Utah 84601.)

Index